CHORD BUILDING

To construct the various chords in this book, use the s

MAJOR — Root, 3rd, & 5th scale tones
MINOR — Root, ♭3rd & 5th
DOMINANT SEVENTH — Root, 3rd, 5th, ♭7th
DIMINISHED — Root, ♭3rd, ♭5th, ♭♭7th
AUGMENTED — Root, 3rd, ♯5th
SIXTH — Root, 3rd, 5th, 6th
MINOR SIXTH — Root, ♭3rd, 5th, 6th
SEVENTH AUGMENTED FIFTH — Root, 3rd, ♯5th, ♭7th
SEVENTH FLAT FIFTH — Root, 3rd, ♭5th, ♭7th
MAJOR SEVENTH — Root, 3rd, 5th, ♮7th
MAJOR SEVENTH FLAT THIRD — Root, ♭3rd, 5th, ♮7th
MINOR SEVENTH — Root, ♭3rd, 5th, ♭7th
MINOR SEVENTH FLAT FIVE — Root, ♭3rd, ♭5th, ♭7th
SEVENTH SUSPENDED FOURTH — Root, 4th, 5th, ♭7th
NINTH — Root, 3rd, 5th, ♭7th, 9th
MAJOR NINTH — Root, 3rd, 5th, ♮7th, 9th
MINOR NINTH — Root, ♭3rd, 5th, ♭7th, 9th
NINTH AUGMENTED FIFTH — Root, 3rd, ♯5th, ♭7th, 9th
NINTH FLAT FIFTH — Root, 3rd, ♭5th, ♭7th, 9th
SEVENTH FLAT NINTH — Root, 3rd, 5th, ♭7th, ♭9th
AUGMENTED NINTH — Root, 3rd, 5th, ♭7th, ♯9th
NINE-SIXTH — Root, 3rd, 5th, 6th, 9th
ELEVENTH — Root, 3rd, 5th, ♭7th, 9th, 11th
AUGMENTED ELEVENTH — Root, 3rd, 5th, ♭7th, 9th, ♯11th
THIRTEENTH — Root, 3rd, 5th, ♭7th, 9th, 11th, 13th

*NOTE — To play chords in higher positions than those pictured, select any chord form, count up 12 frets and play the chord. Any chord form shown in this text can be played 12 frets higher than where it is pictured.

CONTENTS

TUNING THE BANJO

The five open strings of the banjo will be of the same pitch as the five notes shown in the illustration of the piano keyboard.

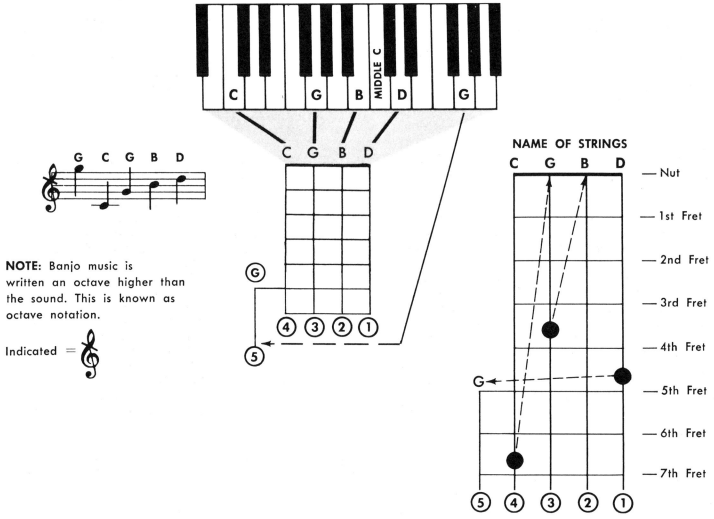

NOTE: Banjo music is written an octave higher than the sound. This is known as octave notation.

Indicated =

BLUEGRASS TUNING

The 5 strings are tuned to a piano as shown.

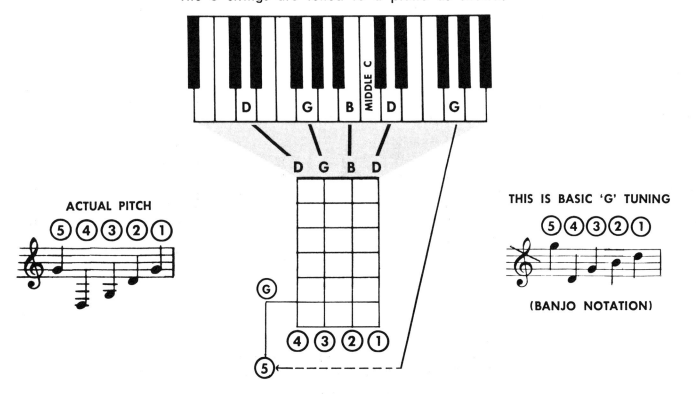

ACTUAL PITCH

THIS IS BASIC 'G' TUNING

(BANJO NOTATION)

BANJO CHORDS

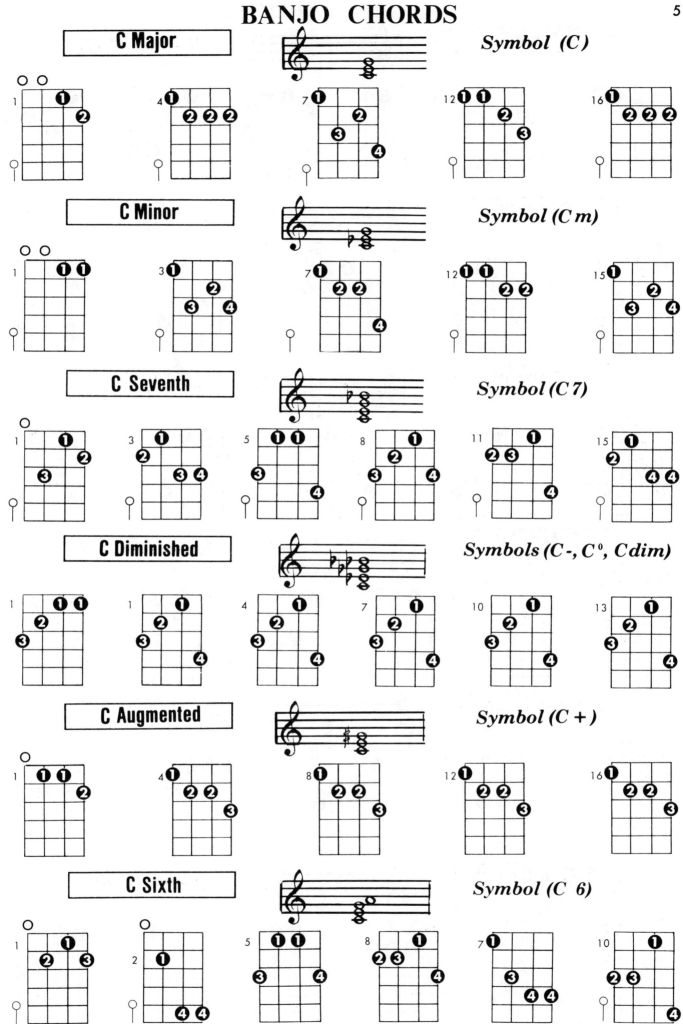

C Major — Symbol (C)

C Minor — Symbol (C m)

C Seventh — Symbol (C 7)

C Diminished — Symbols (C -, C⁰, Cdim)

C Augmented — Symbol (C +)

C Sixth — Symbol (C 6)

BANJO CHORDS

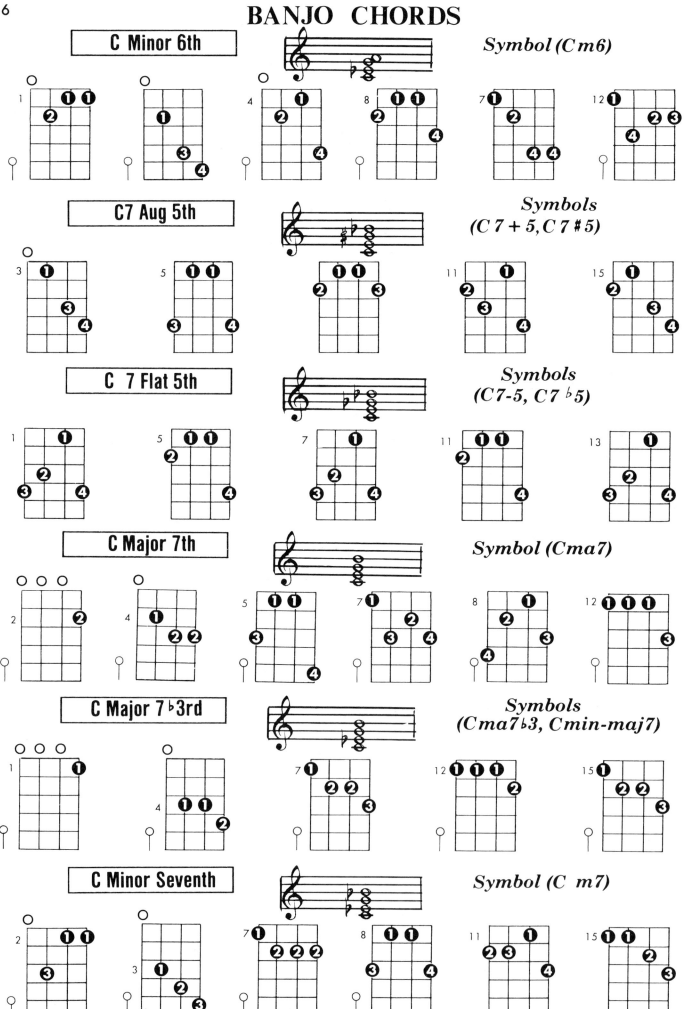

C Minor 6th — *Symbol (Cm6)*

C7 Aug 5th — *Symbols (C 7 + 5, C 7 # 5)*

C 7 Flat 5th — *Symbols (C7-5, C7 ♭5)*

C Major 7th — *Symbol (Cma7)*

C Major 7 ♭3rd — *Symbols (Cma7♭3, Cmin-maj7)*

C Minor Seventh — *Symbol (C m7)*

C Minor 7♭5th

Symbol (C m7♭5)

C7 suspended 4th

Symbol (C 7sus4)

C Ninth

Symbol (C 9)

C Major Ninth

Symbol (C ma 9)

C Minor Ninth

Symbol (C m9)

C 9 Aug 5th

Symbols (C 9 + 5, C 9#5)

BANJO CHORDS

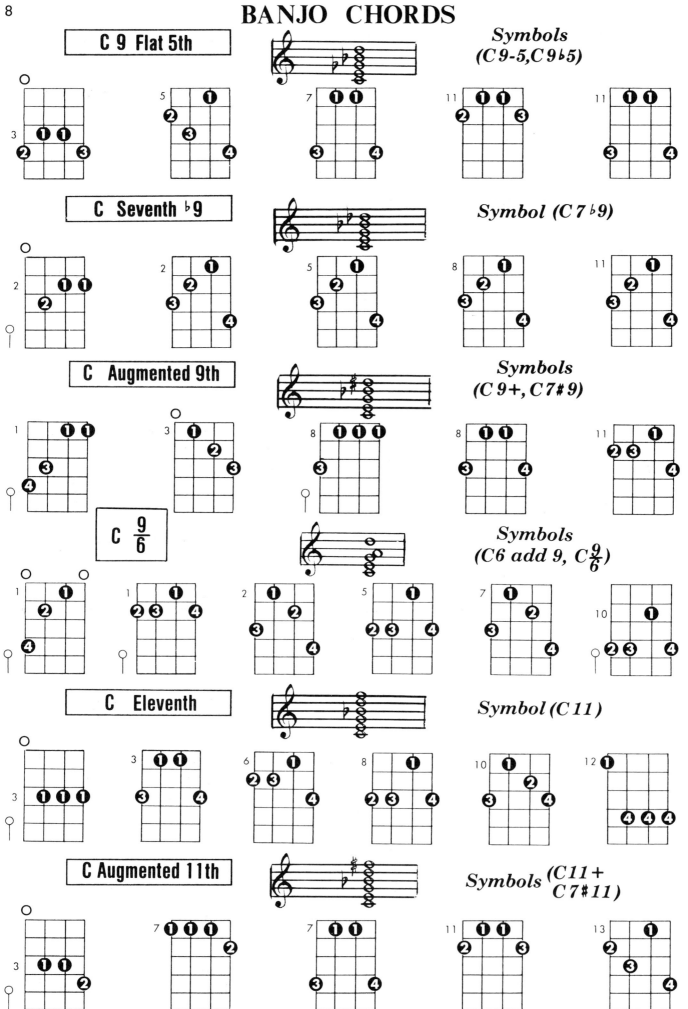

BANJO CHORDS

C Thirteenth

Symbol (C 13)

BANJO CHORDS

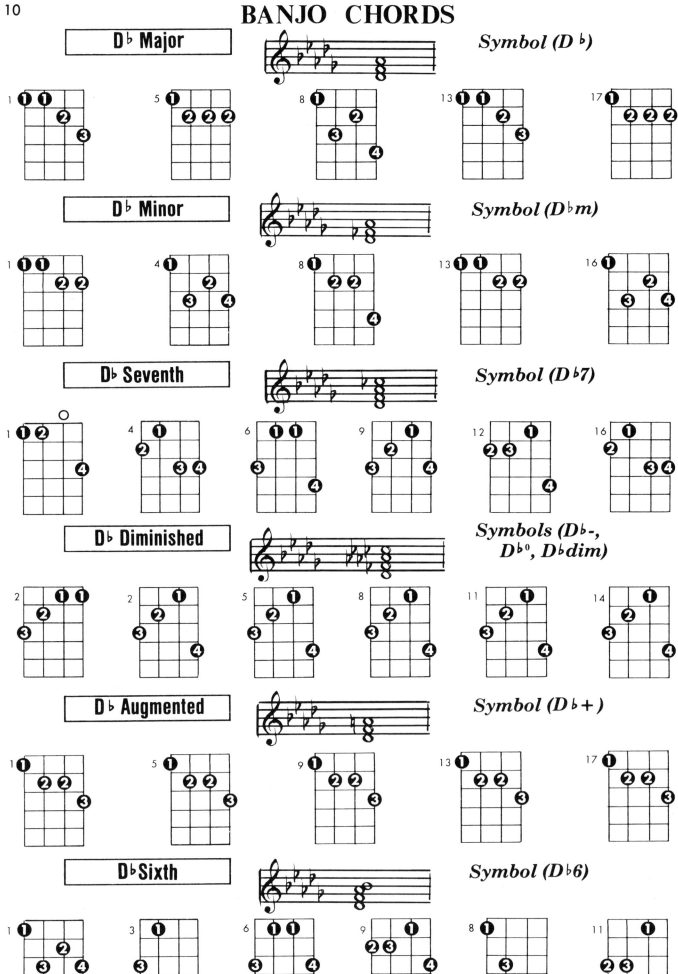

Dᵇ Minor 6th

Symbol (D♭m6)

D♭7 Aug 5th

Symbols (D♭7+5, D♭7♯5)

D♭7 Flat 5th

Symbols (D♭7-5, D♭7♭5)

Dᵇ Major 7th

Symbol (D♭ma7)

Dᵇ Major 7♭3rd

Symbols (D♭ma7♭3, D♭min-maj7)

Dᵇ Minor Seventh

Symbol (D♭m7)

BANJO CHORDS

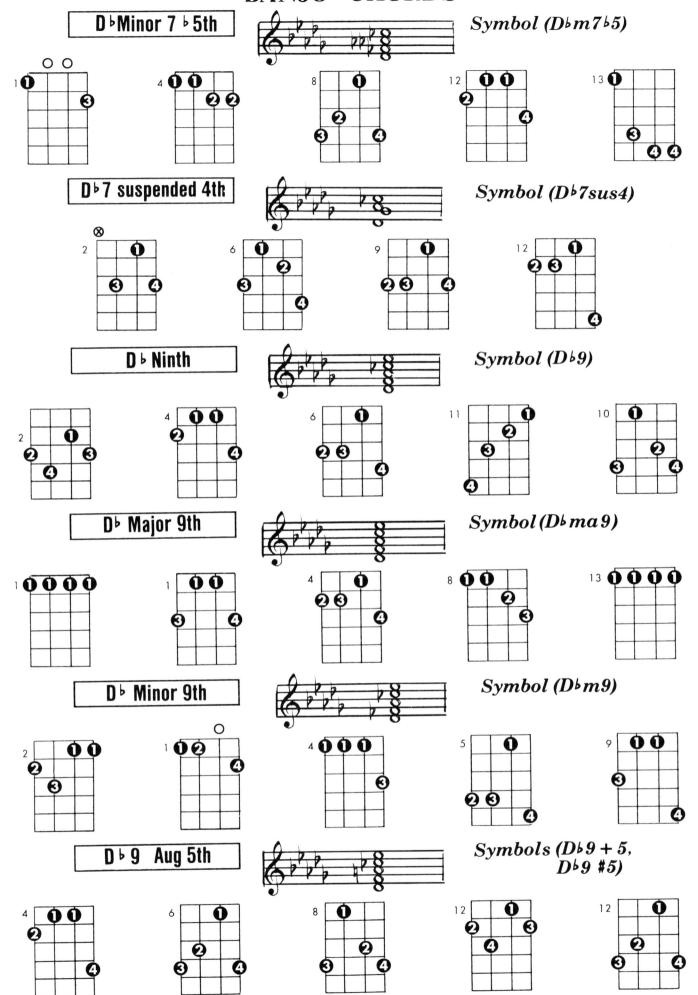

Db Minor 7 b5th — Symbol (Dbm7b5)

Db 7 suspended 4th — Symbol (Db7sus4)

Db Ninth — Symbol (Db9)

Db Major 9th — Symbol (Dbma 9)

Db Minor 9th — Symbol (Dbm9)

Db 9 Aug 5th — Symbols (Db9 + 5, Db9 #5)

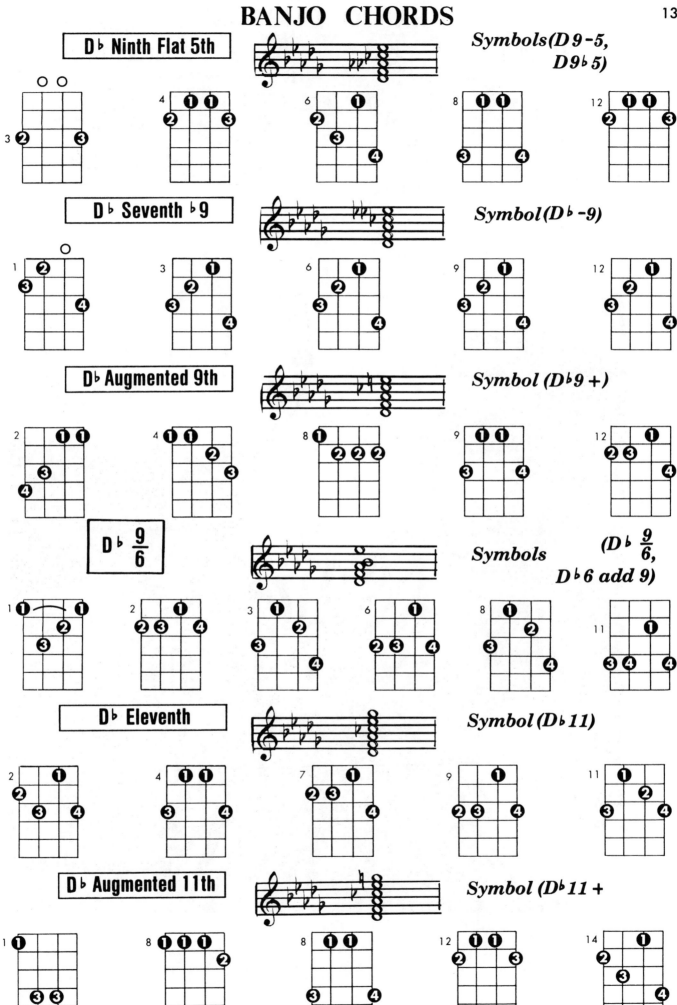

BANJO CHORDS

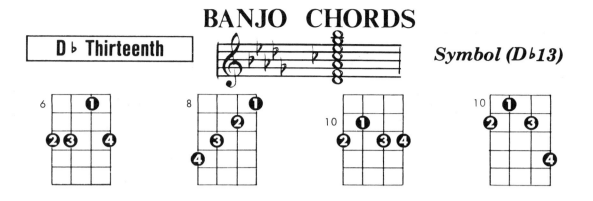

D♭ Thirteenth

Symbol (D♭13)

BANJO CHORDS

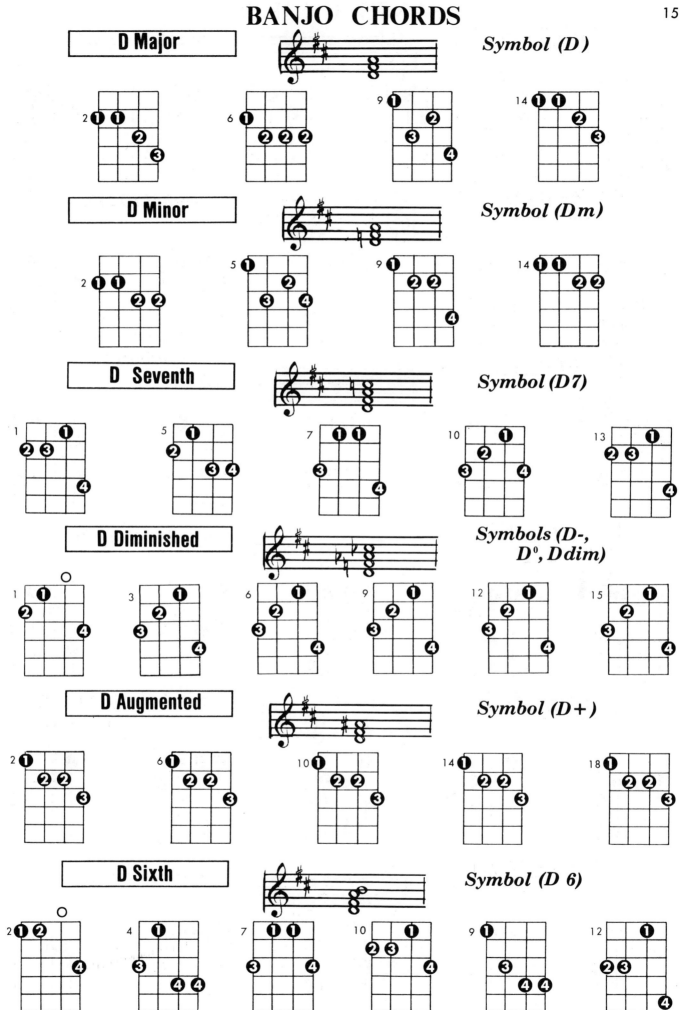

BANJO CHORDS

D Minor 6th

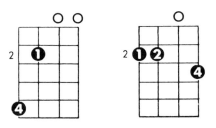

Symbol (D m6)

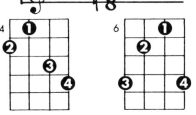
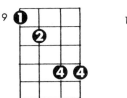

D7 Aug 5th

Symbol (D7+5)

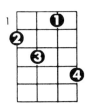
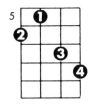

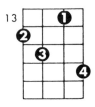

D7 Flat 5th

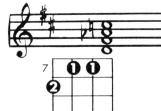

Symbols (D7-5, D7♭5)

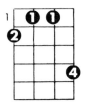
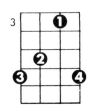
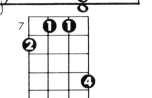
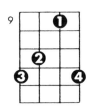
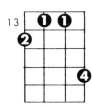

D Major 7th

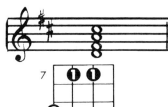

Symbol (Dma7)

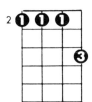
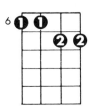
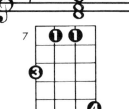
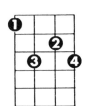
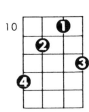

D Major 7♭3rd

Symbols (D ma7♭3, D min-maj7)

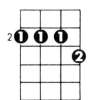
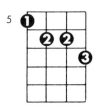

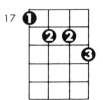

D Minor 7th

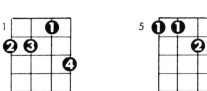

Symbol (D m7)

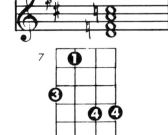
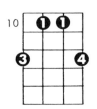
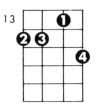

BANJO CHORDS

D Minor 7♭5th
Symbol (Dm7♭5)

D7 suspended 4th
Symbol (D7sus4)

D Ninth
Symbol (D9)

D Major 9th
Symbol (Dma9)

D Minor Ninth
Symbol (Dm9)

D 9 Aug 5th
*Symbols
(D9+5, D9#5)*

BANJO CHORDS

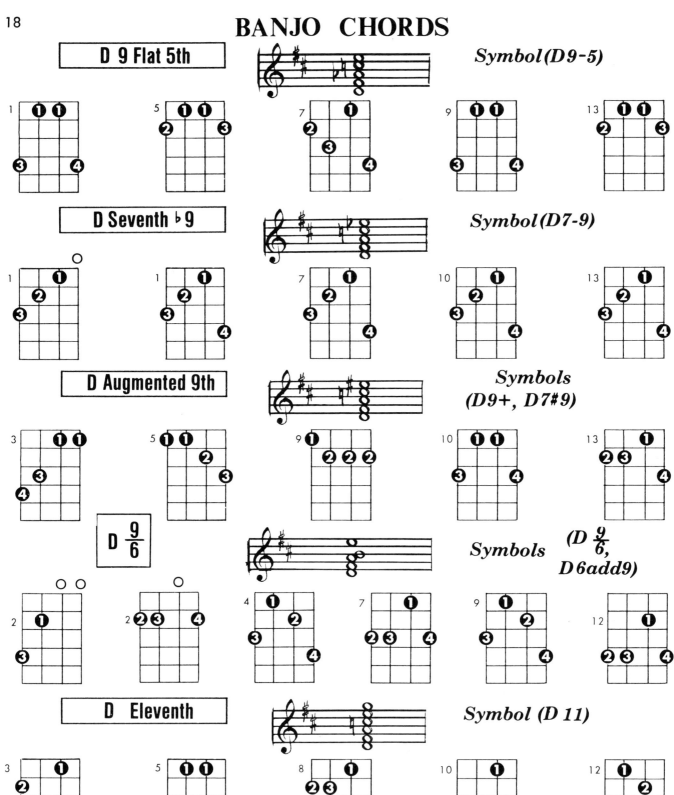

D 9 Flat 5th — *Symbol (D9-5)*

D Seventh ♭9 — *Symbol (D7-9)*

D Augmented 9th — *Symbols (D9+, D7#9)*

$D \frac{9}{6}$ — *Symbols* $(D \frac{9}{6}, D6add9)$

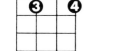

D Eleventh — *Symbol (D 11)*

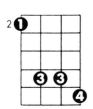
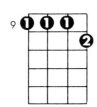

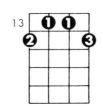
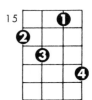

D Augmented 11th — *Symbol (D11 +)*

D Thirteenth

Symbol (D 13)

BANJO CHORDS

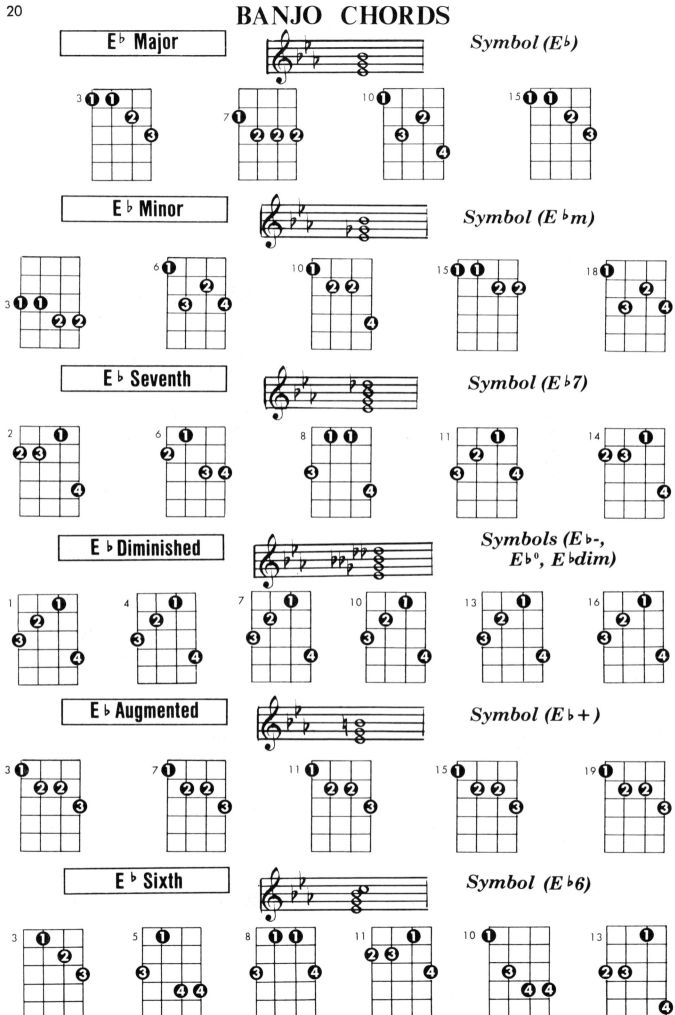

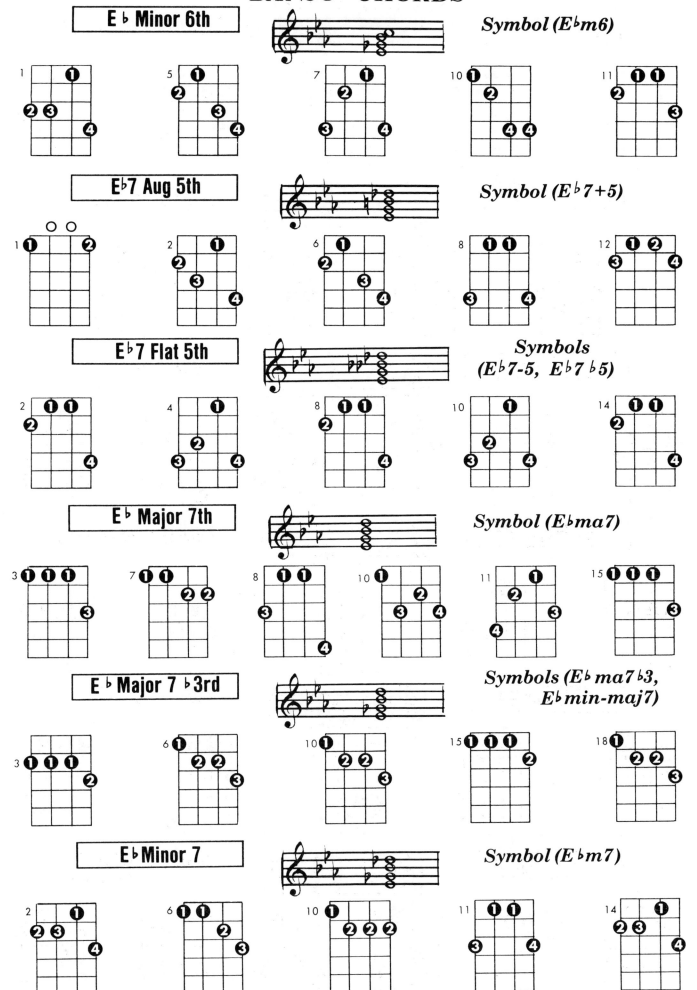

BANJO CHORDS

E♭ Minor 7 ♭5th

Symbol (E♭m7♭5)

E♭7 suspended 4th

Symbol (E♭7sus4)

E♭ Ninth

Symbol (E♭9)

E♭ Major 9th

Symbol (E♭ma 9th)

E♭ Minor 9th

Symbol (E♭m9)

E♭ 9 Aug 5th

*Symbols (E♭ 9#5,
E♭ 9 + 5)*

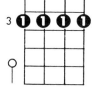
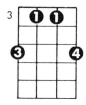
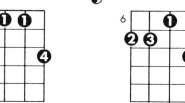
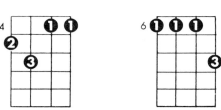
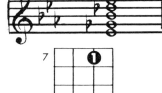
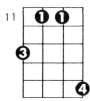

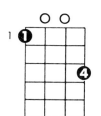
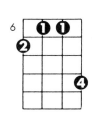

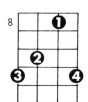
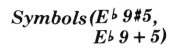
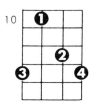
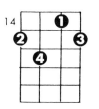

BANJO CHORDS

E♭9 Flat 5th

Symbol (E♭9-5)

E♭ Seventh ♭9

Symbol (E♭7-9)

E♭ Augmented 9th

Symbols
(E♭9 + , E♭7#9)

E♭ 9/6

Symbols
(E♭ 9/6, E♭6add9)

E♭ Eleventh

Symbol (E♭11)

E♭ Augmented 11th

Symbol (E♭11 +)

BANJO CHORDS

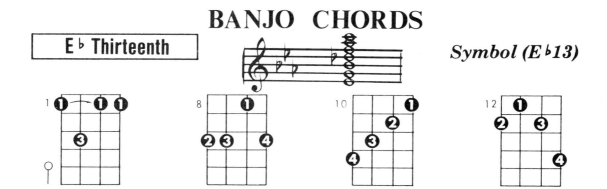

E♭ Thirteenth

Symbol (E♭13)

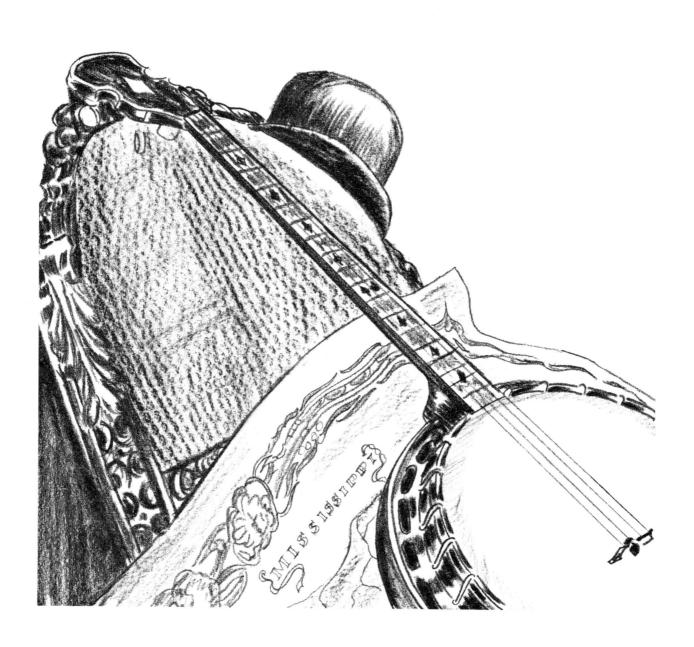

BANJO CHORDS

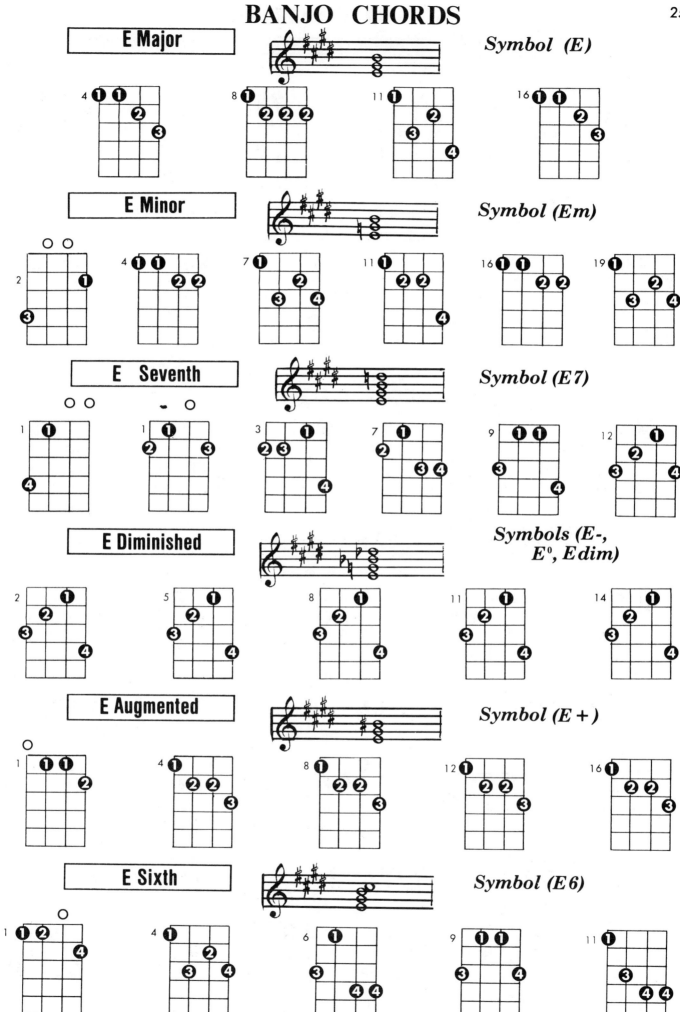

BANJO CHORDS

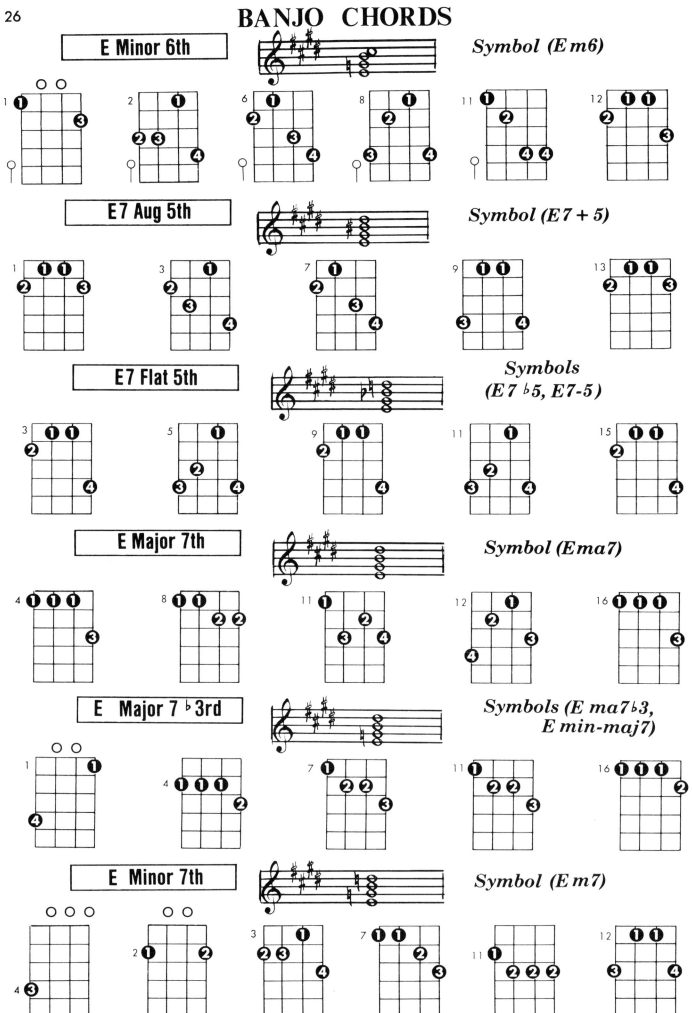

E Minor 6th — Symbol (E m6)

E7 Aug 5th — Symbol (E7 + 5)

E7 Flat 5th — Symbols (E7 ♭5, E7-5)

E Major 7th — Symbol (Ema7)

E Major 7 ♭3rd — Symbols (E ma7♭3, E min-maj7)

E Minor 7th — Symbol (E m7)

BANJO CHORDS

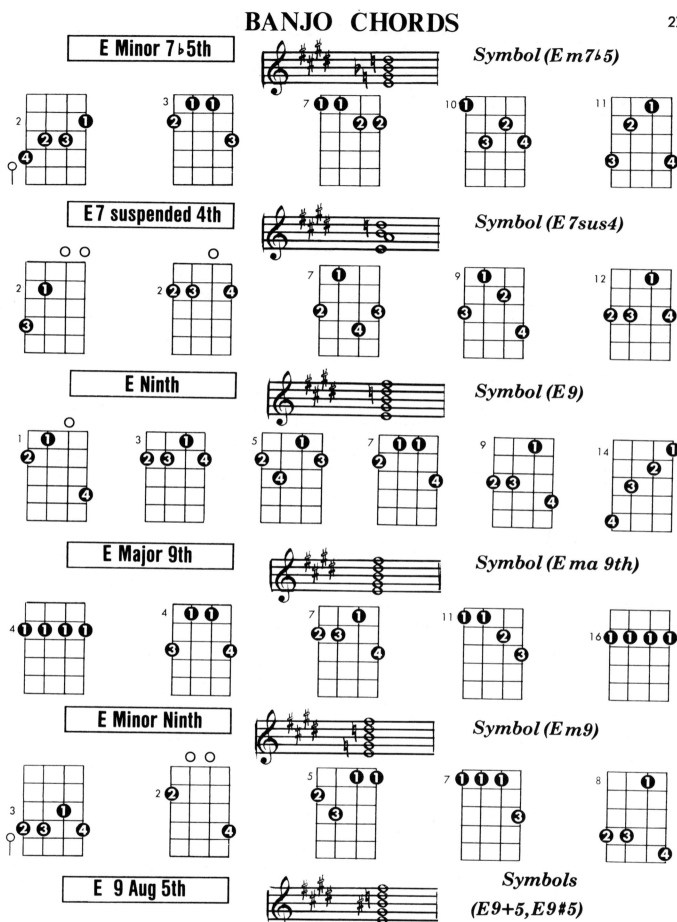

E Minor 7♭5th — Symbol (E m7♭5)

E 7 suspended 4th — Symbol (E 7sus4)

E Ninth — Symbol (E 9)

E Major 9th — Symbol (E ma 9th)

E Minor Ninth — Symbol (E m9)

E 9 Aug 5th — Symbols (E9+5, E9♯5)

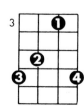
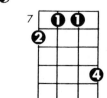
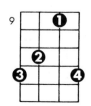

BANJO CHORDS

Symbol (E 9-5)

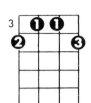
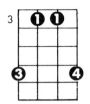
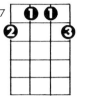
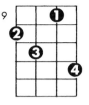
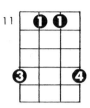

Symbol (E 7-9)

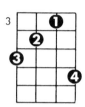

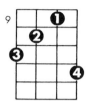
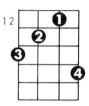

Symbols (E 9+, E 7#9)

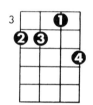
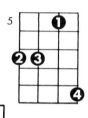
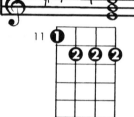
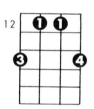
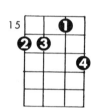

Symbols (E $\frac{9}{6}$, E6add9)

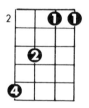
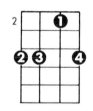
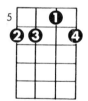
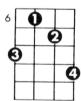
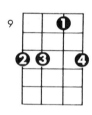
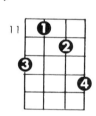

Symbol (E11)

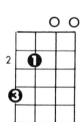
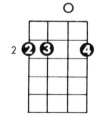

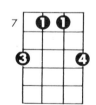
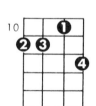

Symbol (E 11 +)

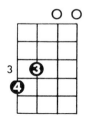
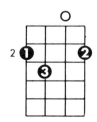
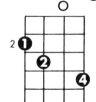
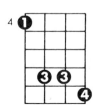
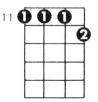

E Thirteenth

Symbol (E 13)

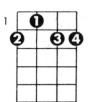
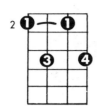
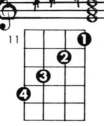
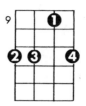
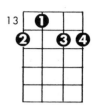

BANJO CHORDS

F Major

Symbol (F)

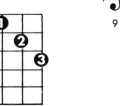
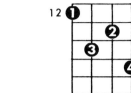
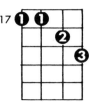

F Minor

Symbol (F m)

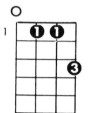
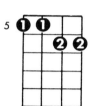

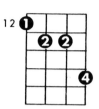
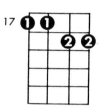

F Seventh

Symbol (F 7)

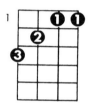
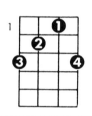

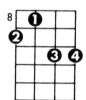
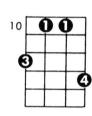
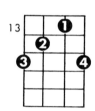

F Diminished

Symbols (F -, F⁰, F dim)

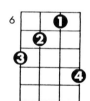
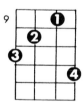
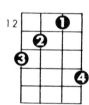

F Augmented

Symbol (F +)

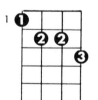
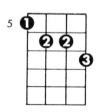

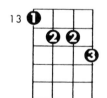
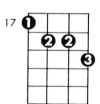

F Sixth

Symbol (F 6)

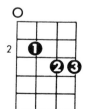
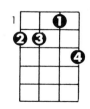

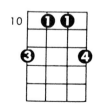
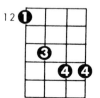

BANJO CHORDS

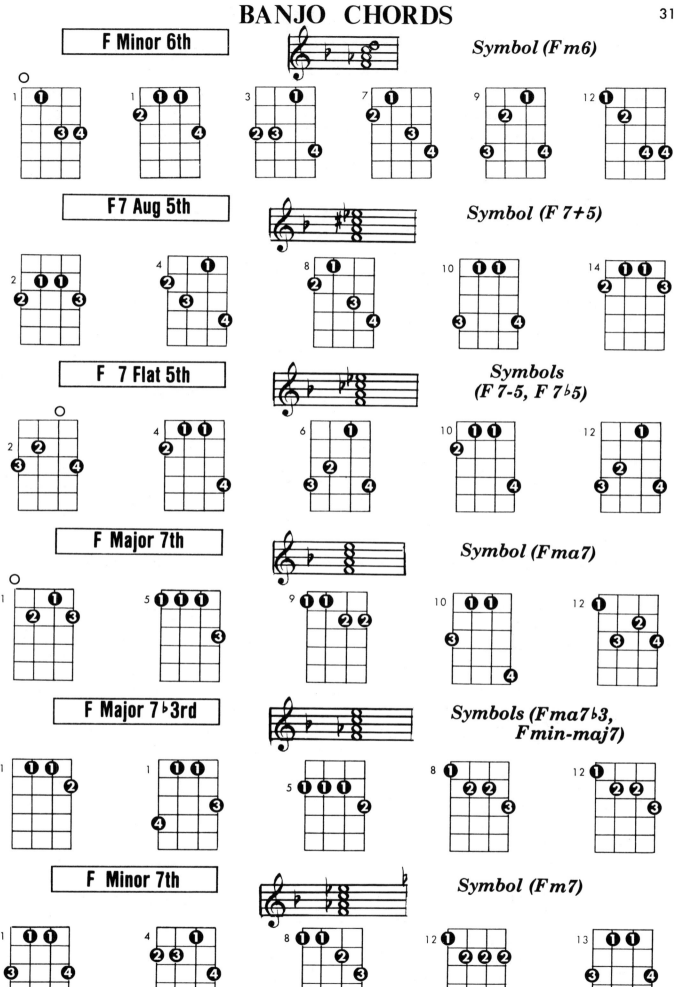

BANJO CHORDS

F Minor 7♭5th

Symbol (Fm7♭5)

F7 suspended 4th

Symbol (F 7sus4)

F Ninth

Symbol (F 9)

F Minor 9th

Symbol (F m9)

F Major 9th

Symbol (F ma9)

F9 Aug 5th

Symbols (F 9 + 5, F 9 #5)

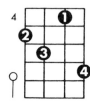

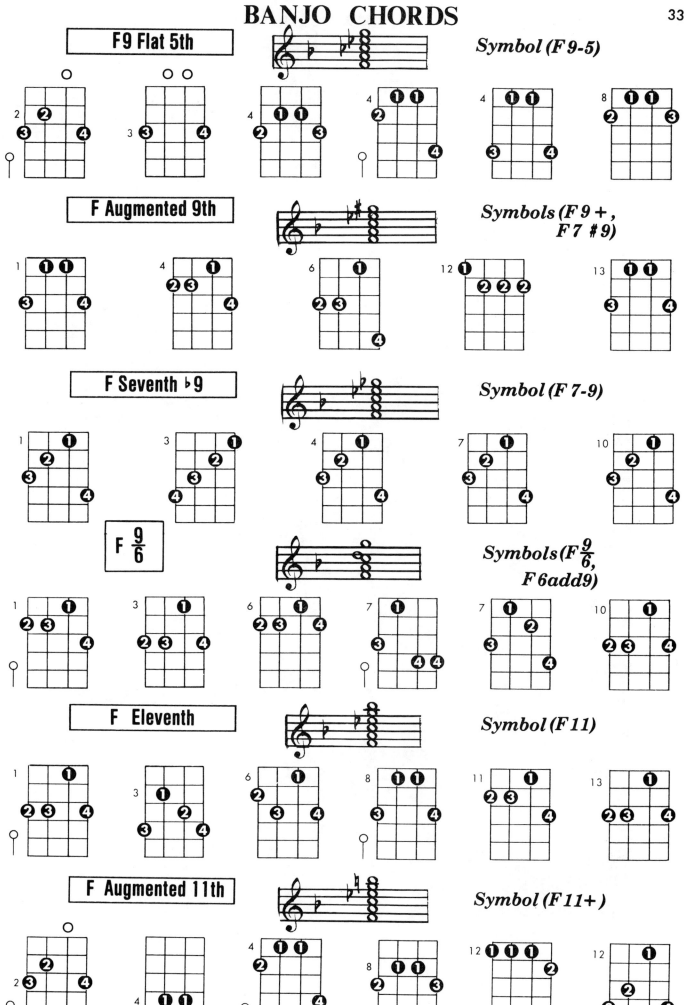

BANJO CHORDS

F Thirteenth

Symbol (F 13)

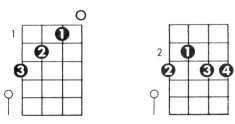

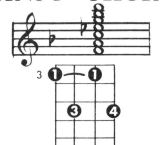

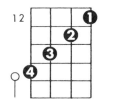

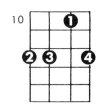

BANJO CHORDS

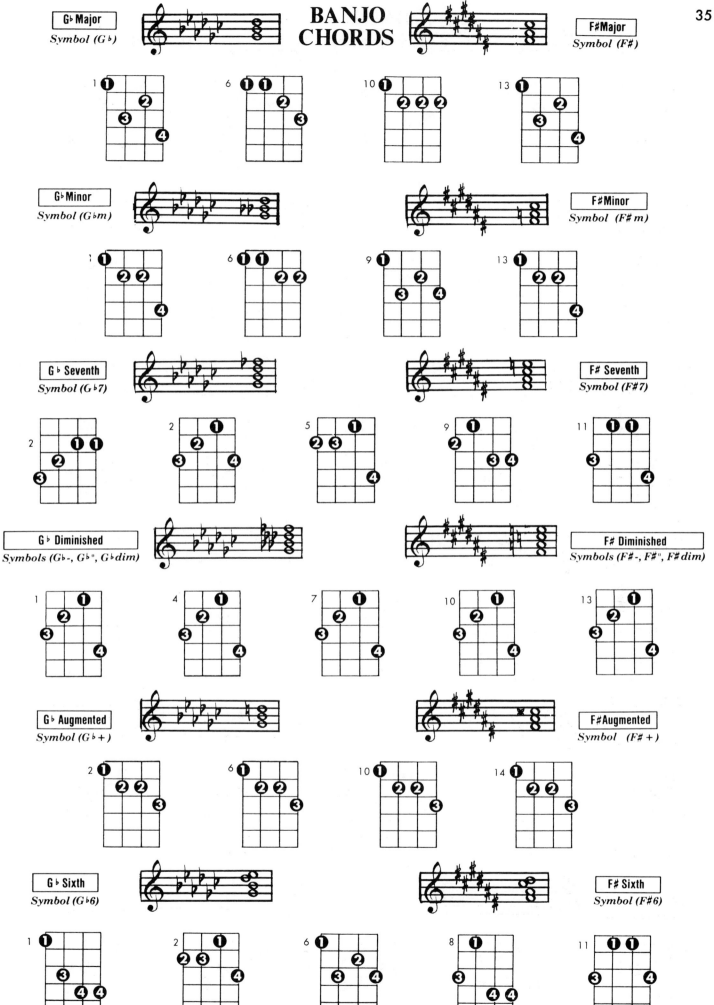

BANJO CHORDS

G♭ Minor 6th
Symbol (G♭m6)

F# Minor 6th
Symbol (F#m6)

G♭7 Aug 5th
Symbol (G♭7 + 5)

F#7 Aug 5th
Symbol (F# 7+5)

G♭ 7 Flat 5th
Symbols (G♭7-5, G♭7♭5)

F# 7 Flat 5th
Symbols (F# 7-5, F# 7♭5)

G♭ Major 7th
Symbol (G♭ma7)

F# Major 7th
Symbol (F#ma7)

G♭ Major 7 ♭3rd
Symbols (G♭ma7♭3, G♭min-maj7)

F # Major 7 ♭3rd
Symbols (F#ma7♭3, F#min-maj7)

G♭ Minor Seventh
Symbol (G♭m7)

F# Minor 7th
Symbol (F#m7)

BANJO CHORDS

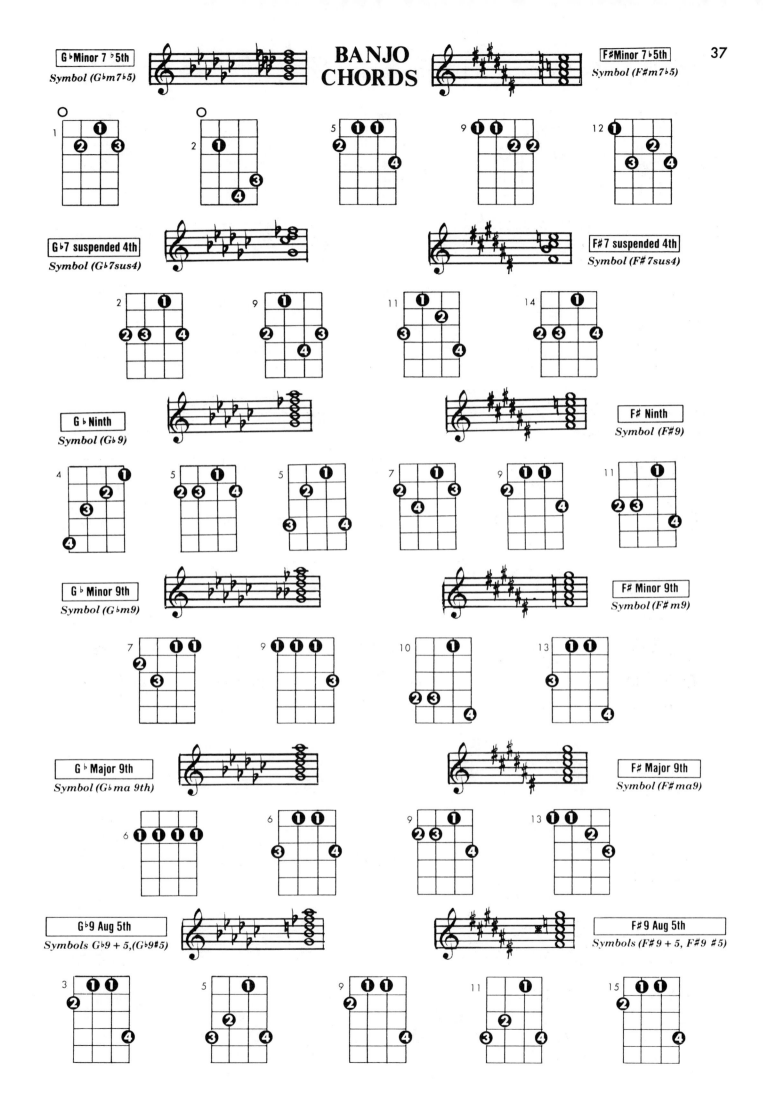

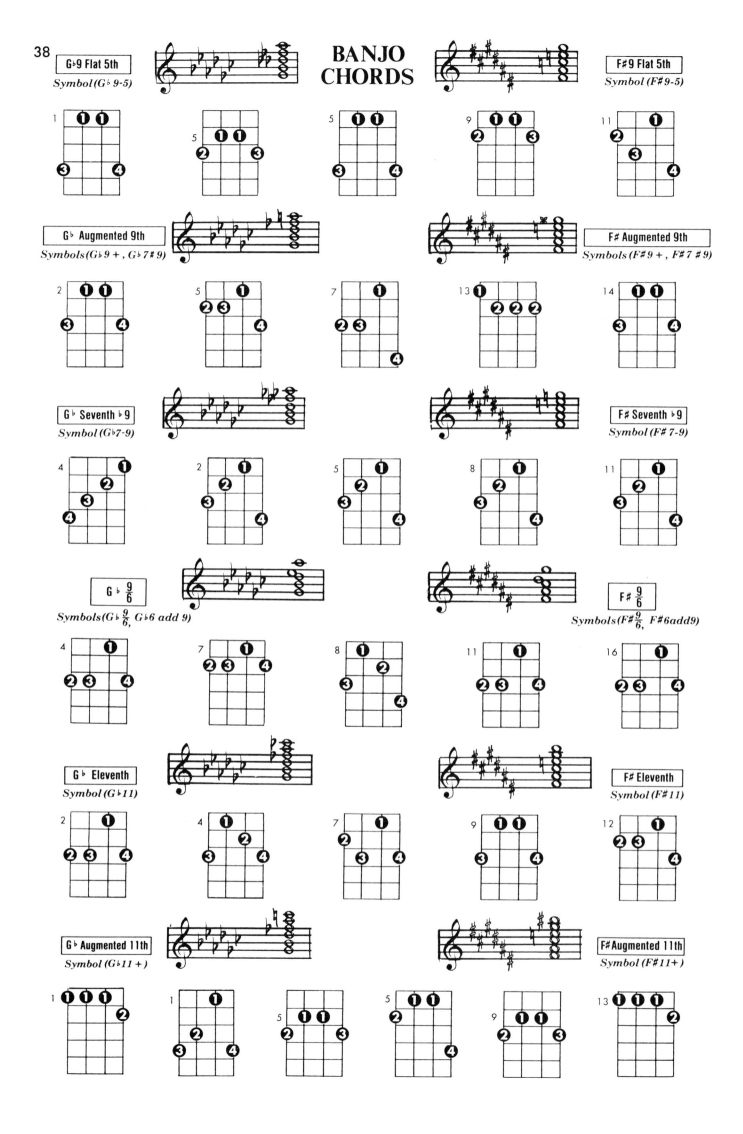

BANJO CHORDS

G♭ Thirteenth
Symbol (G♭13)

F♯ Thirteenth
Symbol (F♯13)

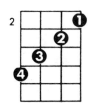
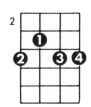
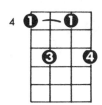
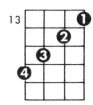
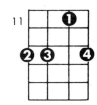

BANJO CHORDS

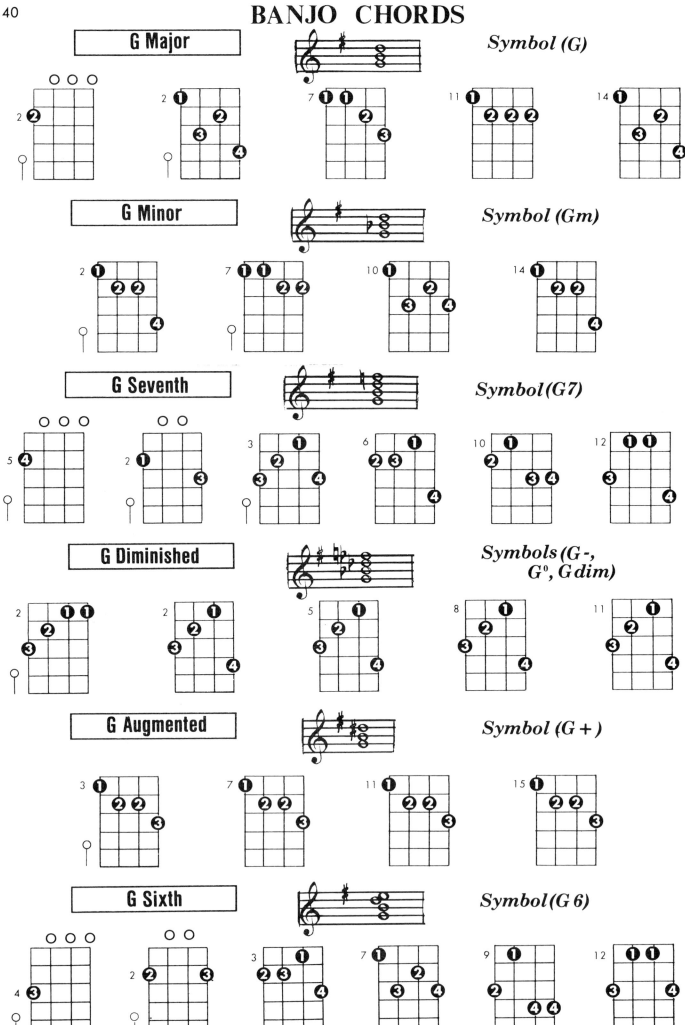

G Minor 6th

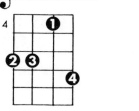

Symbol (Gm6)

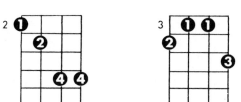

G7 Aug 5th

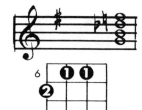

Symbol (G7 + 5)

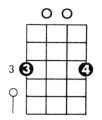
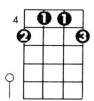
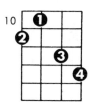
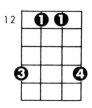

G7 Flat 5th

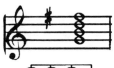
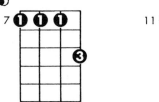

Symbols (G7-5, G7♭5)

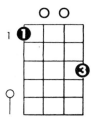
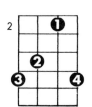
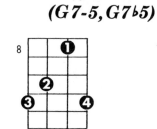
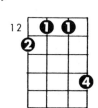

G Major Seventh

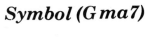

Symbol (Gma7)

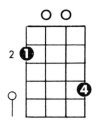
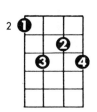

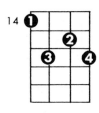

G Major 7♭3rd

Symbols (Gma7♭3, G min-maj7)

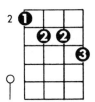
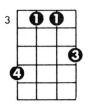
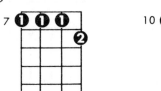

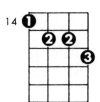

G Minor Seventh

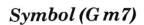

Symbol (Gm7)

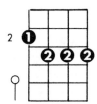
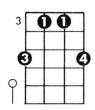

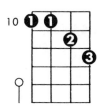
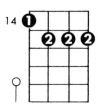

BANJO CHORDS

G Minor 7♭5th

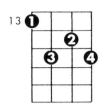

Symbol (Gm7♭5)

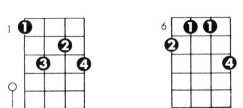 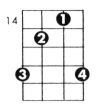

G7 suspended 4th

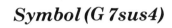

Symbol (G 7sus4)

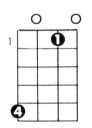 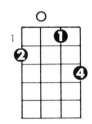 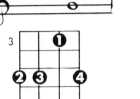 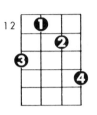 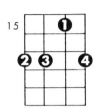

G Ninth

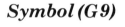

Symbol (G 9)

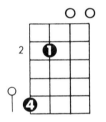 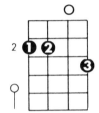 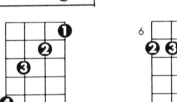 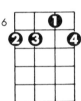 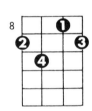

G 9 Aug 5th

*Symbols
(G 9 + 5, G 9 #5)*

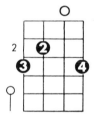 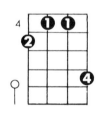 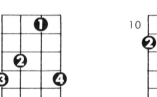 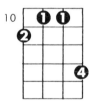 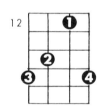

G Minor Ninth

Symbol (G m9)

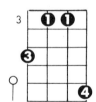 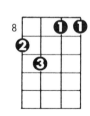 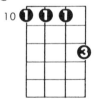 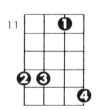 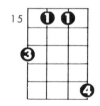

G Major Ninth

Symbol (G ma 9)

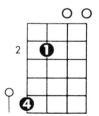 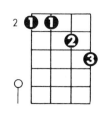 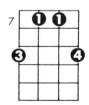 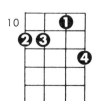

BANJO CHORDS

G 9 Flat 5th

Symbol (G9-5)

G Augmented 9th

Symbols (G 9 +, G 7 # 9)

G Seventh ♭9

Symbol (G7-9)

$G \dfrac{9}{6}$

Symbols (G $\dfrac{9}{6}$, G6add9)

G Eleventh

Symbol (G 11)

G Augmented 11th

Symbol (G 11 +)

BANJO CHORDS

G Thirteenth   *Symbol (G 13)*

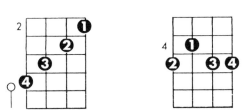
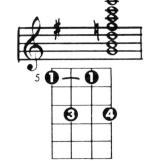
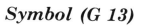
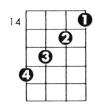
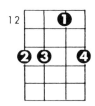

BANJO CHORDS

A♭ Major

Symbol (A♭maj)

A♭ Minor

Symbol (A♭m)

A♭ Seventh

Symbol (A♭7)

A♭ Diminished

Symbols (A♭-, A♭⁰, A♭dim)

A♭ Augmented

Symbol (A♭+)

A♭ Sixth

Symbol (A♭6)

BANJO CHORDS

A♭ Minor 6th

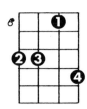
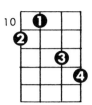

Symbol (A♭m6)

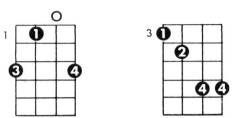

A♭7 Aug 5th

Symbol (A♭7 + 5)

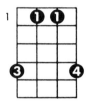

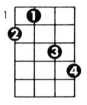
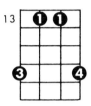

A♭7 Flat 5th

Symbols (A♭7-5, A♭7♭5)

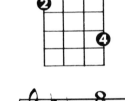

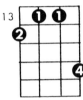

A♭ Major 7th

Symbol (A♭ma7)

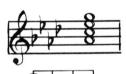
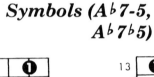

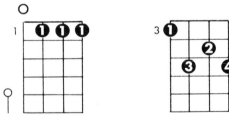
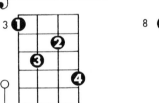

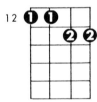

A♭ Major 7 ♭3rd

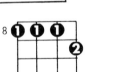

Symbols (A♭ma7♭3, A♭min-maj7)

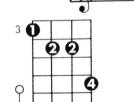
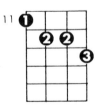

A♭ Minor 7th

Symbol (A♭m7)

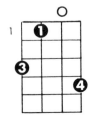
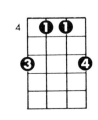

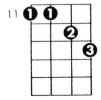
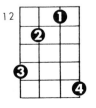

A♭ Minor 7 ♭5th

Symbol (A♭m7♭5)

A♭7 suspended 4th

Symbol (A♭7sus4)

A♭ Ninth

Symbol (A♭9)

A♭ Minor 9th

Symbol (A♭m9)

A♭ Major 9th

Symbol (A♭ma 9th)

A♭9 Aug 5th

Symbols (A♭9 + 5, A♭9 #5)

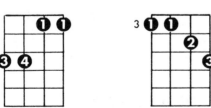
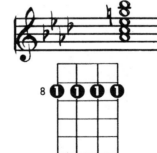
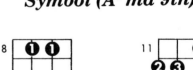
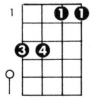
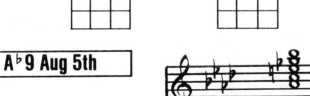
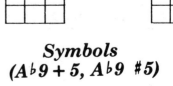
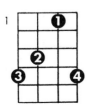
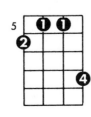
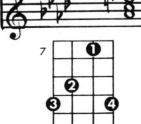
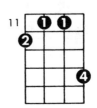
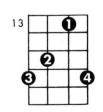

BANJO CHORDS

A♭ 9 Flat 5th

Symbol (A♭9-5)

 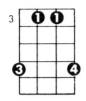   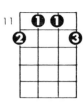

A♭ Seventh ♭9

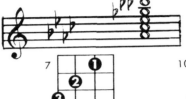

Symbol (A♭7-9)

  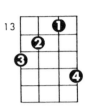

A♭ Augmented 9th

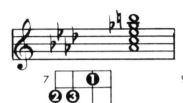 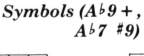

Symbols (A♭9 +, A♭7 #9)

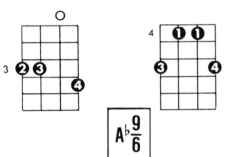

$A♭\frac{9}{6}$

Symbols (A♭$\frac{9}{6}$, A♭6 add 9)

A♭ Eleventh

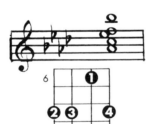

Symbol (A♭11)

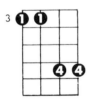

A♭ Augmented 11th

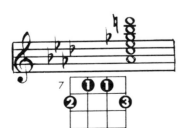

Symbol (A♭11 +)

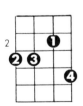 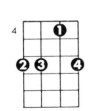 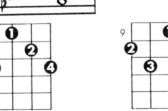 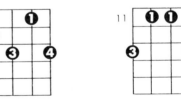

 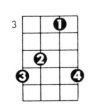 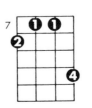

A♭ Thirteenth

Symbol (A♭13)

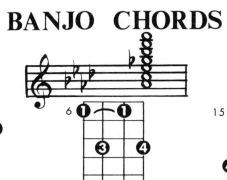

BANJO CHORDS

A Major

Symbol (A)

A Minor

Symbol (Am)

A Seventh

Symbol (A7)

A Diminished

Symbols (A-, A⁰, Adim)

A Augmented

Symbol (A +)

A Sixth

Symbol (A6)

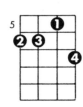

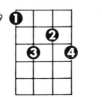

BANJO CHORDS

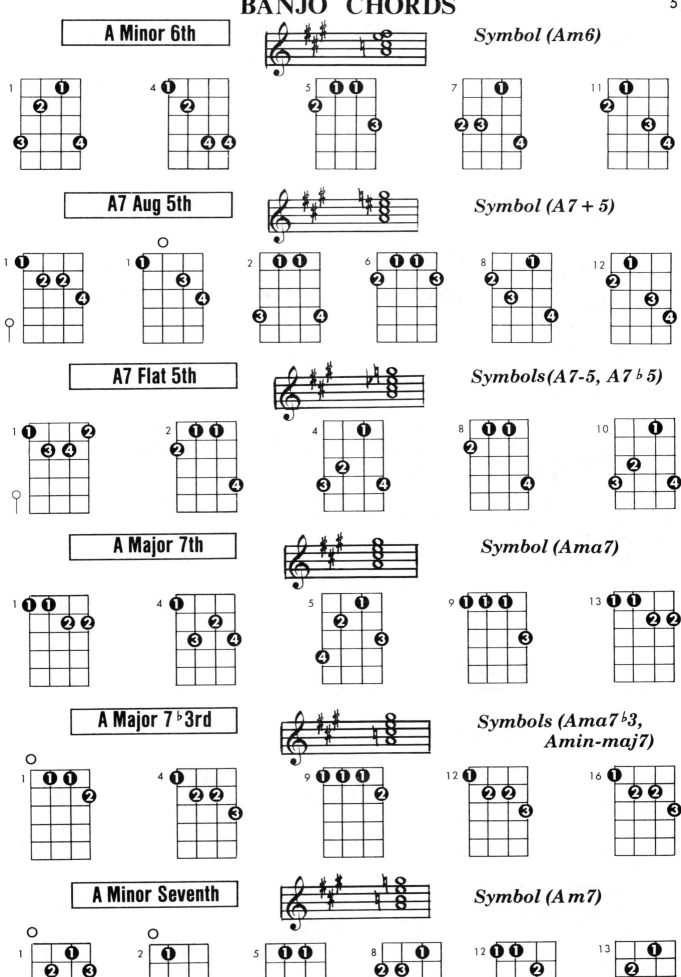

BANJO CHORDS

A Minor 7♭5th

Symbol (Am7♭5)

A7 suspended 4th

Symbol (A7sus4)

A Ninth

Symbol (A9)

A Minor Ninth

Symbol (Am9)

A Major 9th

Symbol (Ama9)

A9 Aug 5th

Symbols (A9 + 5, A9 #5)

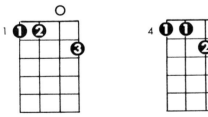
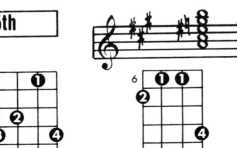
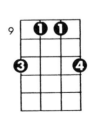

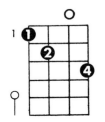
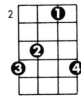
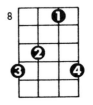
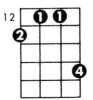

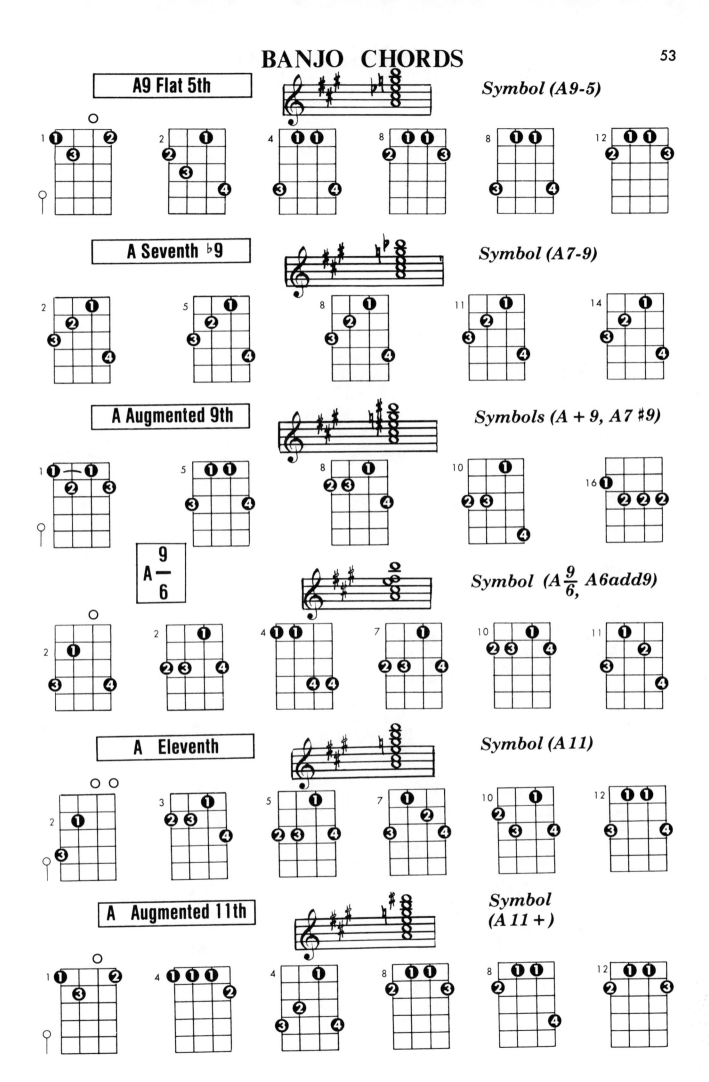

BANJO CHORDS

| A   Thirteenth |

Symbol (A 13)

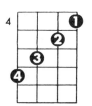
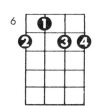
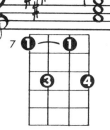
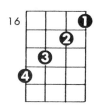
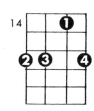

BANJO CHORDS

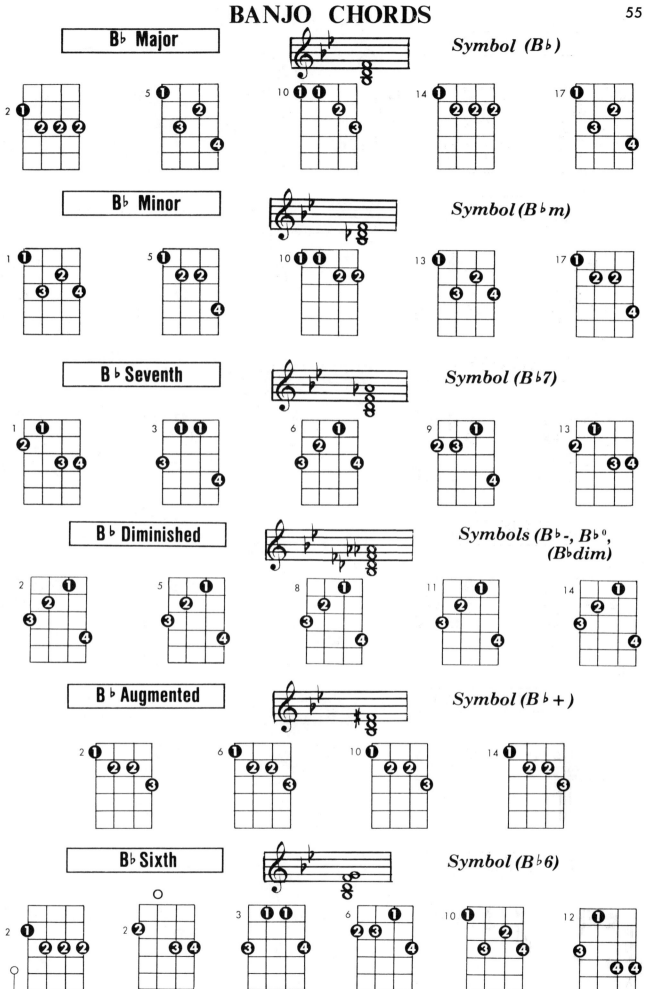

B♭ Major — Symbol (B♭)

B♭ Minor — Symbol (B♭m)

B♭ Seventh — Symbol (B♭7)

B♭ Diminished — Symbols (B♭-, B♭⁰, (B♭dim)

B♭ Augmented — Symbol (B♭+)

B♭ Sixth — Symbol (B♭6)

BANJO CHORDS

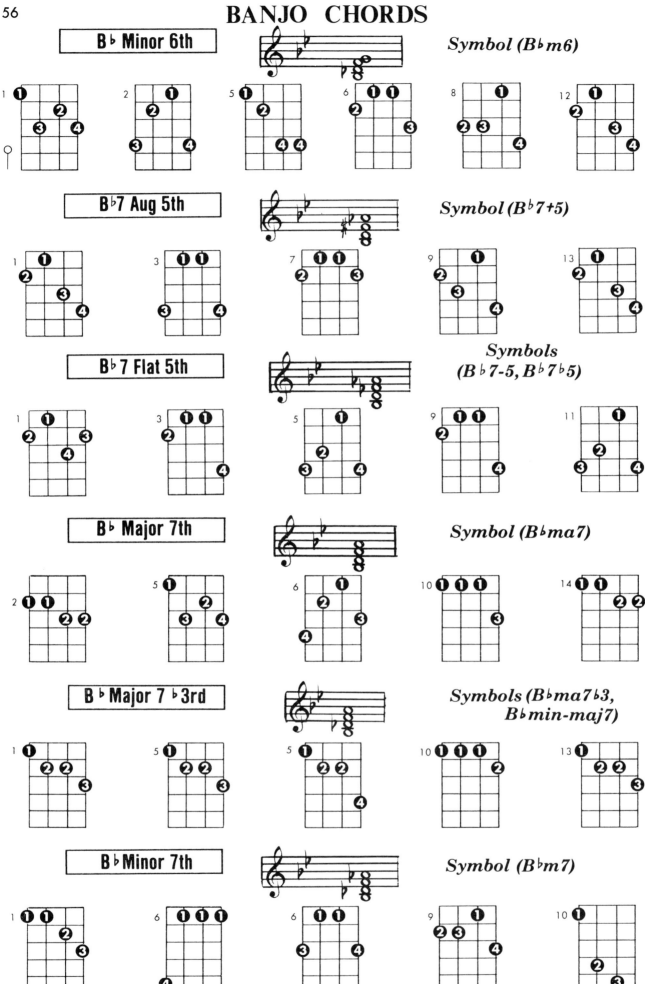

Bᵇ Minor 6th *Symbol (Bᵇm6)*

Bᵇ7 Aug 5th *Symbol (Bᵇ7+5)*

Bᵇ 7 Flat 5th *Symbols (Bᵇ7-5, Bᵇ7ᵇ5)*

Bᵇ Major 7th *Symbol (Bᵇma7)*

Bᵇ Major 7 ᵇ3rd *Symbols (Bᵇma7ᵇ3, Bᵇmin-maj7)*

Bᵇ Minor 7th *Symbol (Bᵇm7)*

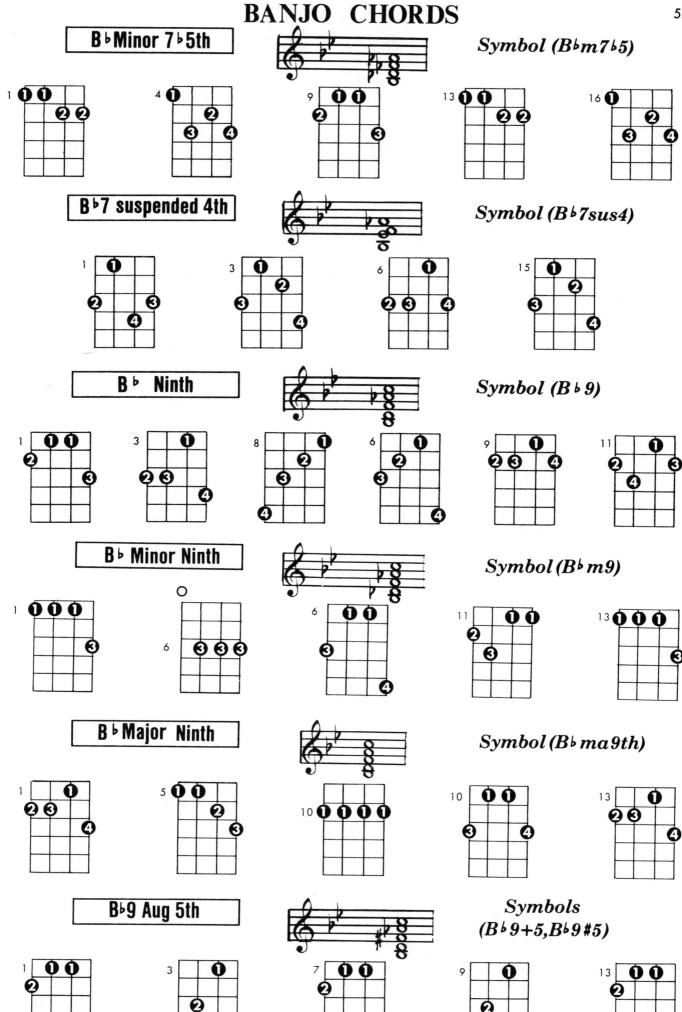

BANJO CHORDS

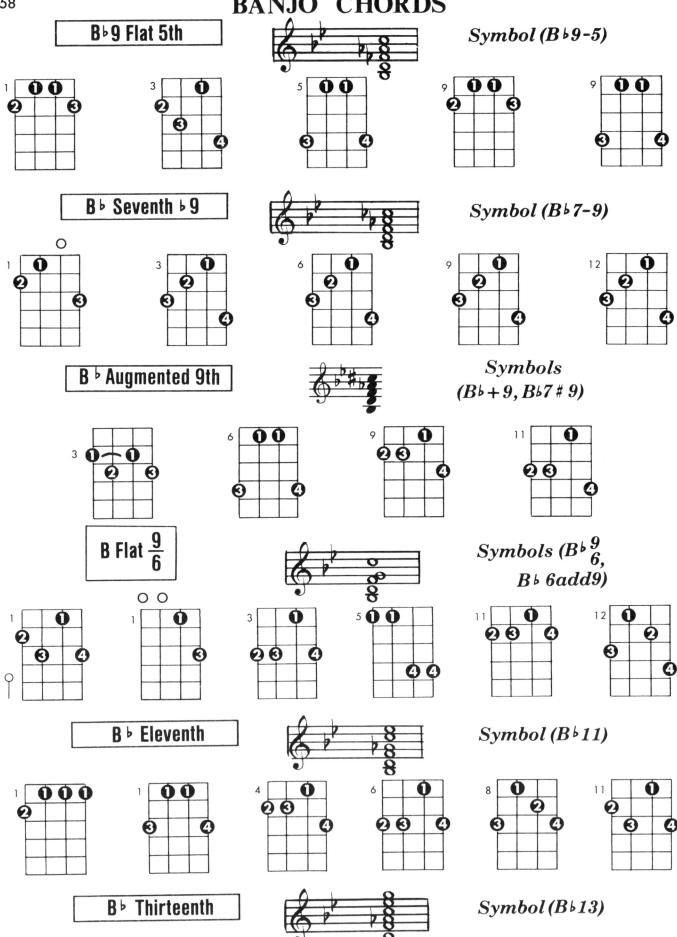

B♭9 Flat 5th — *Symbol (B♭9-5)*

B♭ Seventh ♭9 — *Symbol (B♭7-9)*

B♭ Augmented 9th — *Symbols (B♭+9, B♭7♯9)*

B Flat ⁹⁄₆ — *Symbols (B♭ ⁹⁄₆, B♭ 6add9)*

B♭ Eleventh — *Symbol (B♭11)*

B♭ Thirteenth — *Symbol (B♭13)*

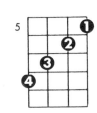
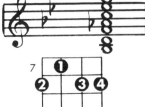
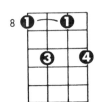
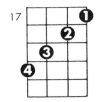

BANJO CHORDS

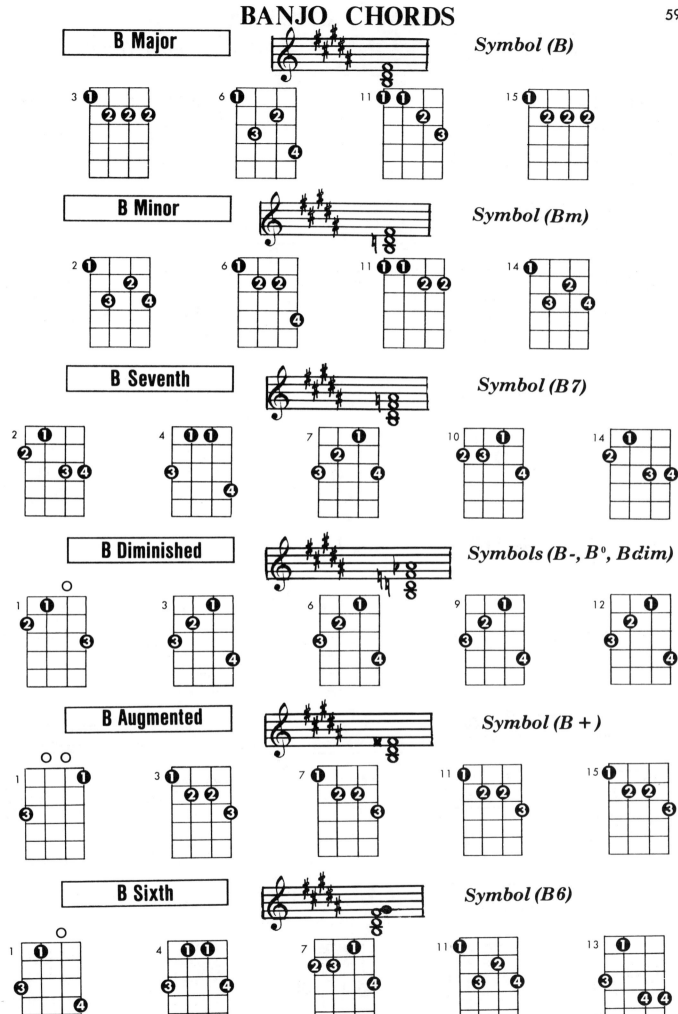

BANJO CHORDS

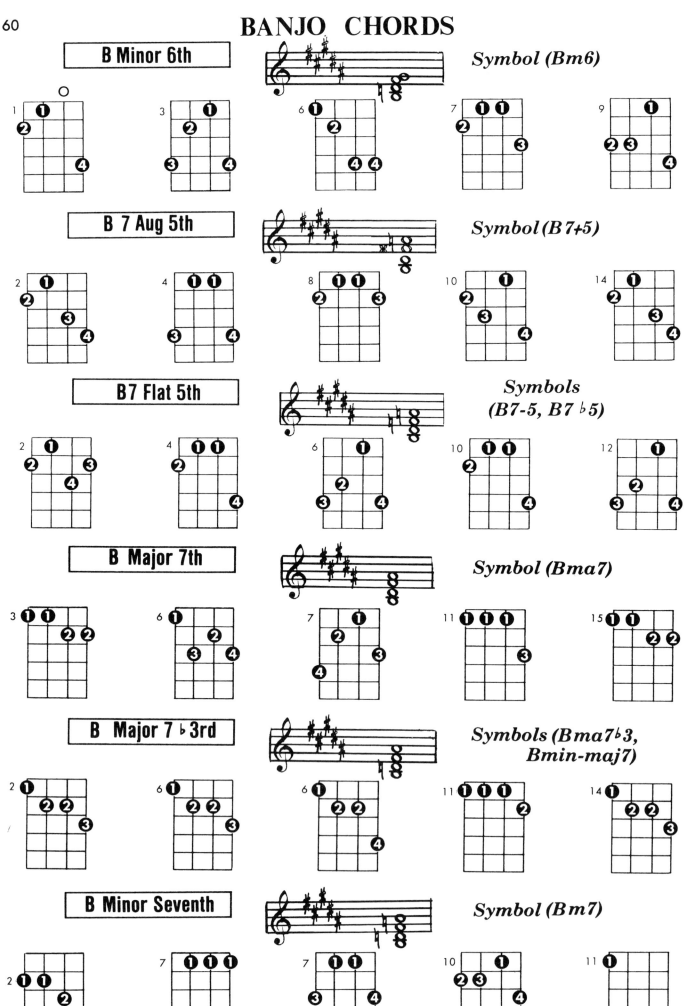

BANJO CHORDS

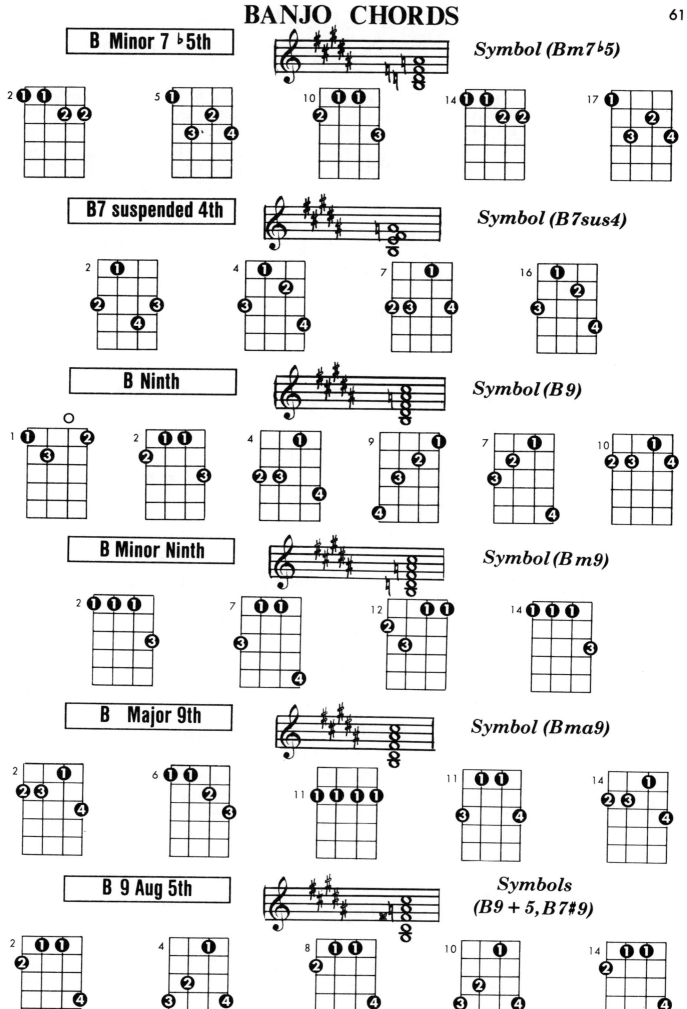

BANJO CHORDS

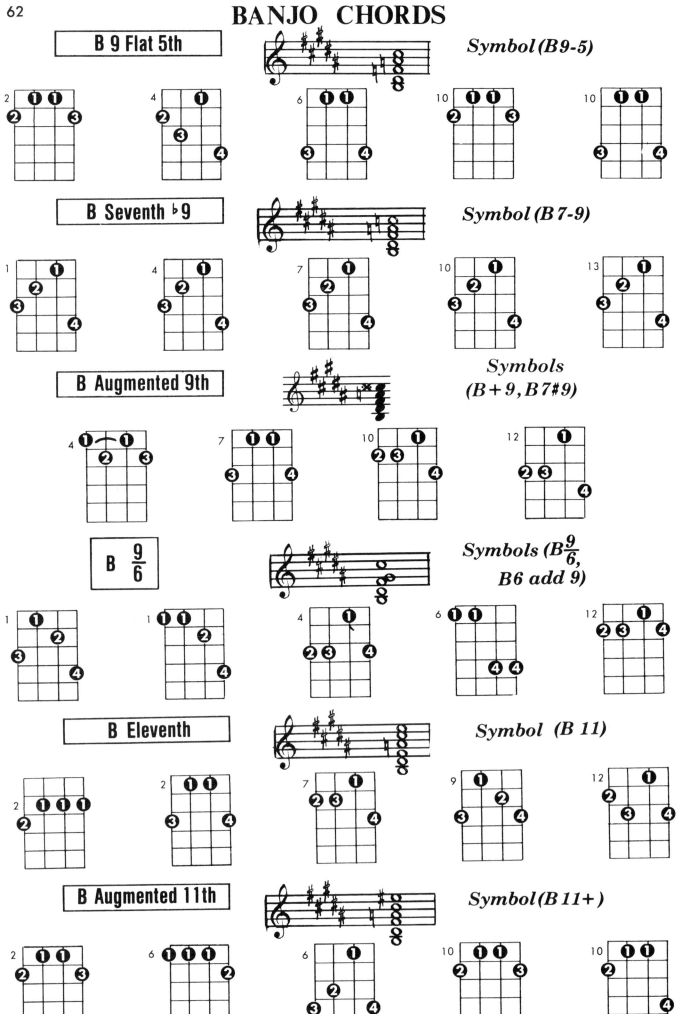

B 9 Flat 5th

Symbol (B9-5)

B Seventh ♭9

Symbol (B7-9)

B Augmented 9th

Symbols (B+9, B7#9)

B 9/6

Symbols (B 9/6, B6 add 9)

B Eleventh

Symbol (B 11)

B Augmented 11th

Symbol (B 11+)

B Thirteenth

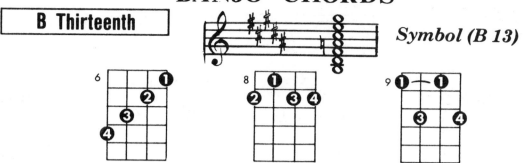

Symbol (B 13)

BLUEGRASS BANJO CHORDS

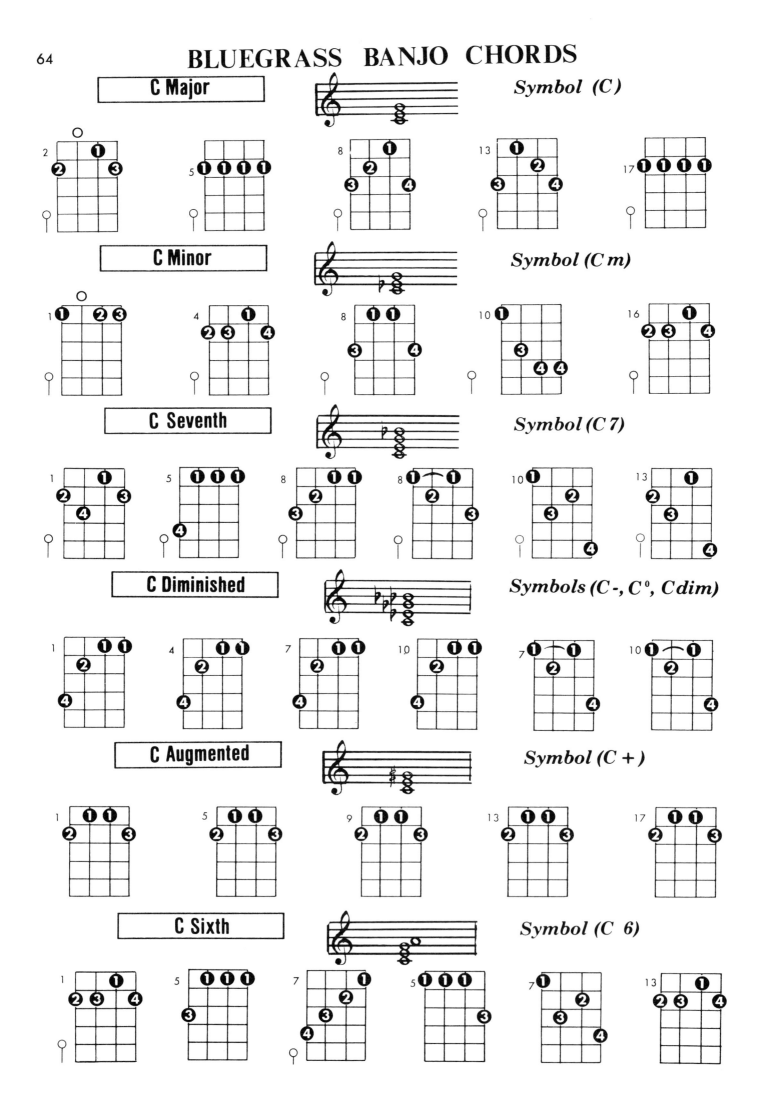

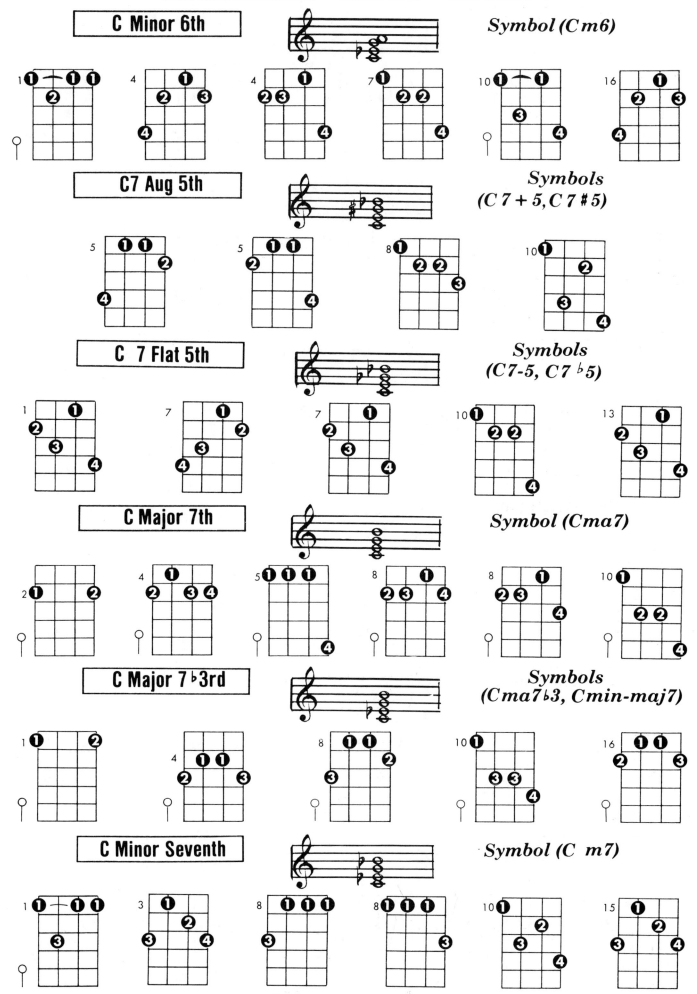

BLUEGRASS BANJO CHORDS

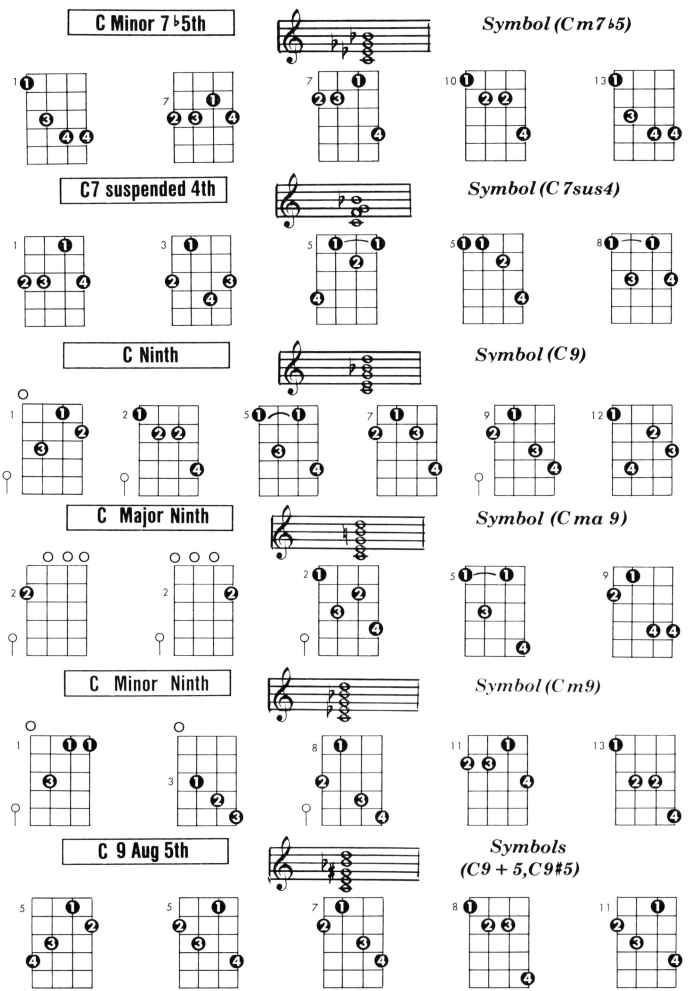

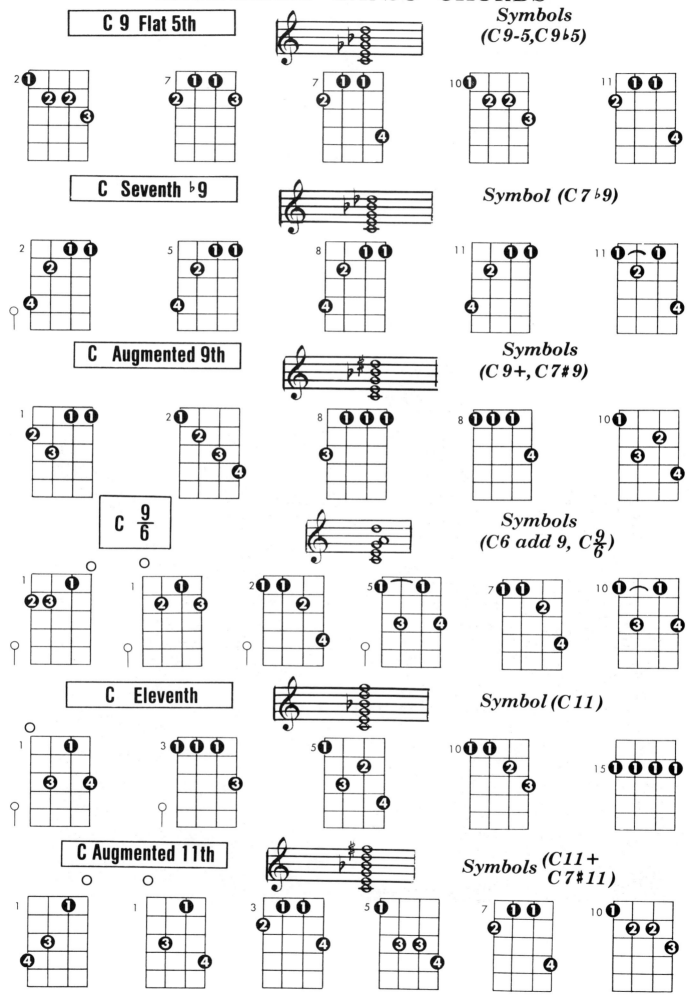

BLUEGRASS BANJO CHORDS

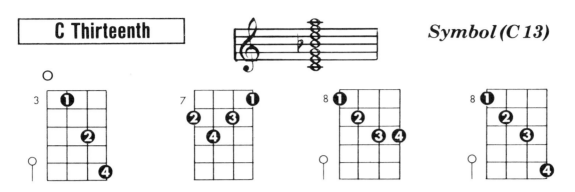

C Thirteenth

Symbol (C 13)

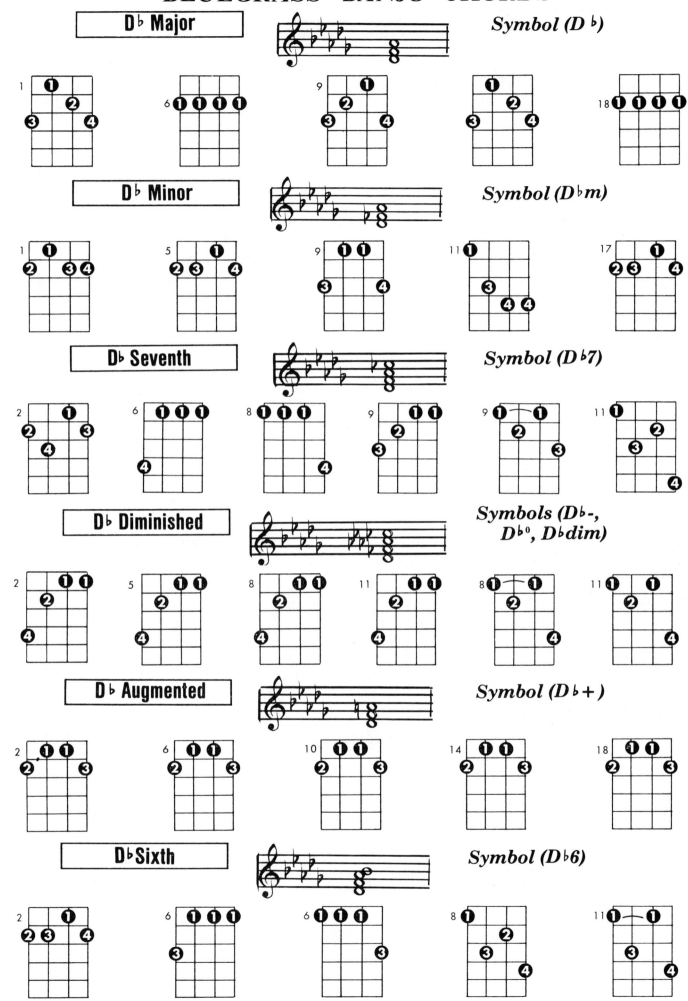

BLUEGRASS BANJO CHORDS

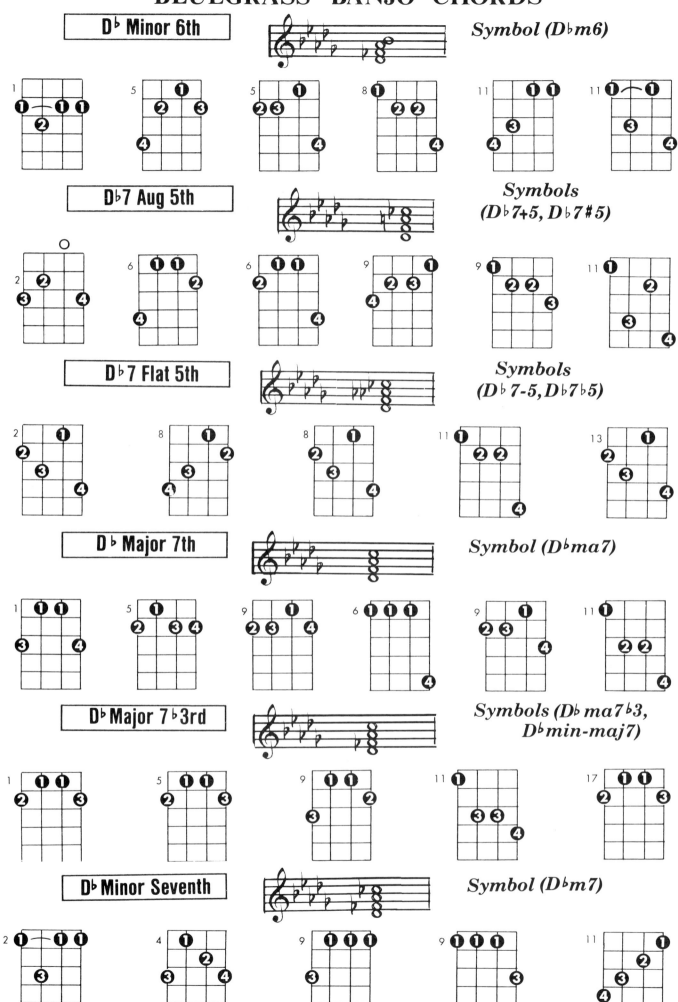

D♭ Minor 6th

Symbol (D♭m6)

D♭7 Aug 5th

Symbols (D♭7+5, D♭7#5)

D♭7 Flat 5th

Symbols (D♭7-5, D♭7♭5)

D♭ Major 7th

Symbol (D♭ma7)

D♭ Major 7♭3rd

Symbols (D♭ma7♭3, D♭min-maj7)

D♭ Minor Seventh

Symbol (D♭m7)

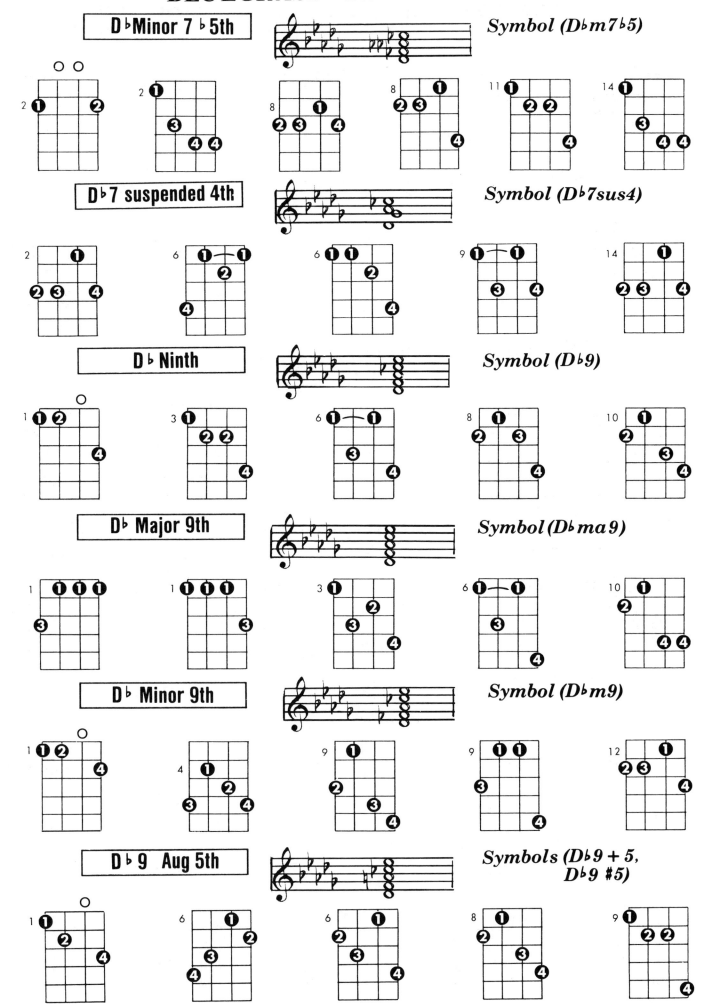

BLUEGRASS BANJO CHORDS

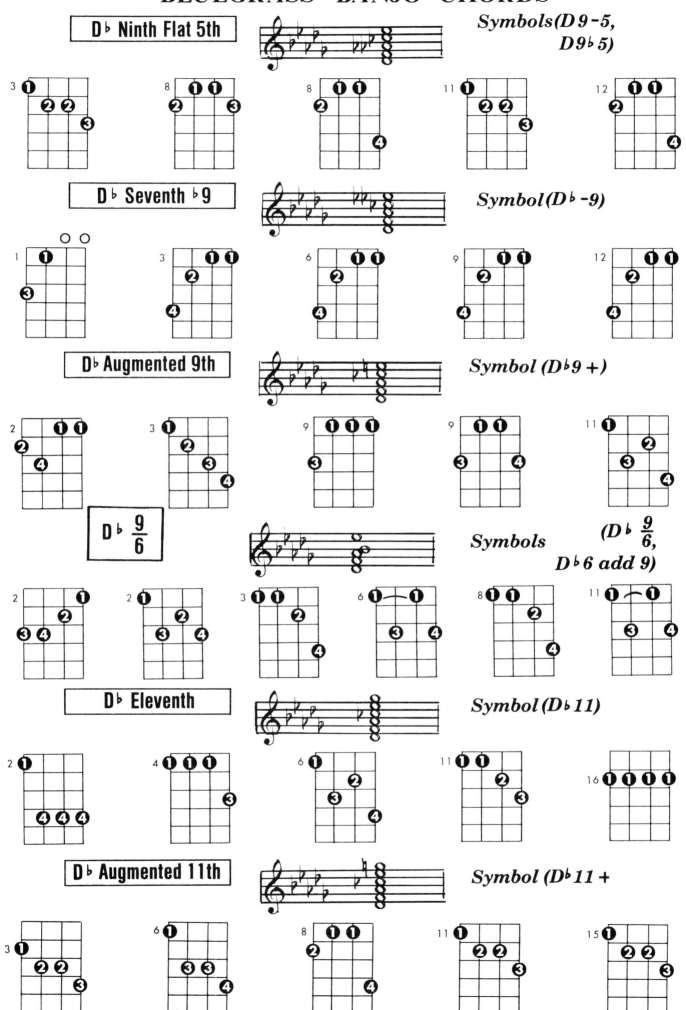

D♭ Thirteenth

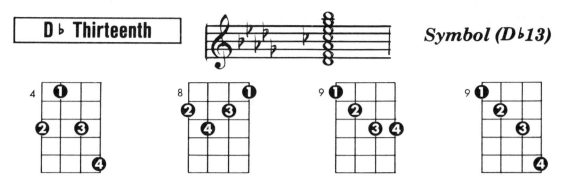

Symbol (D♭13)

BLUEGRASS BANJO CHORDS

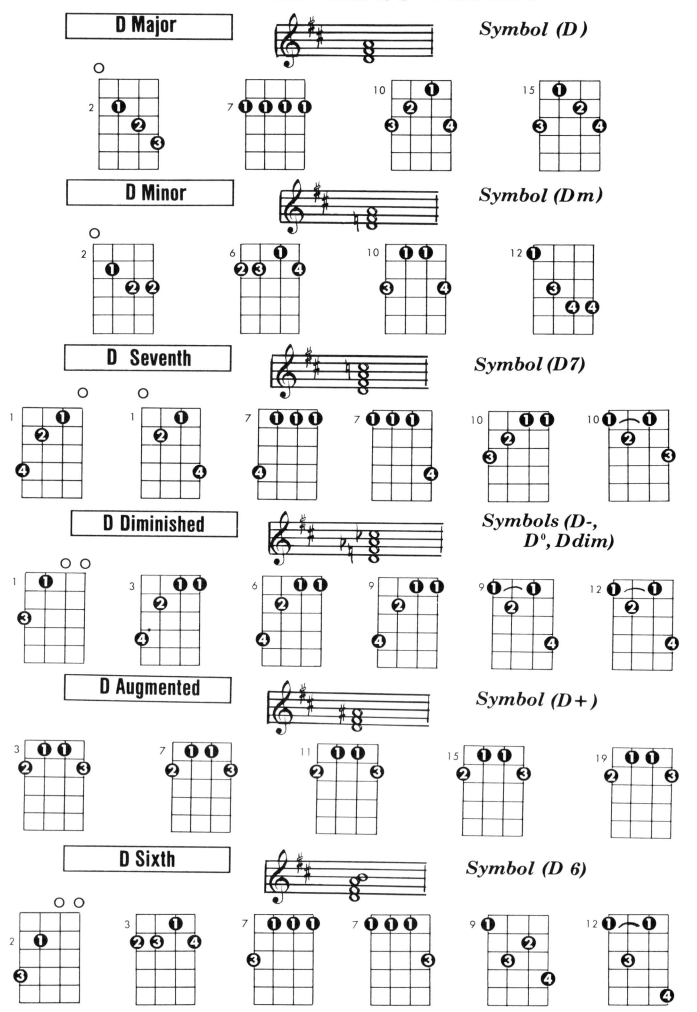

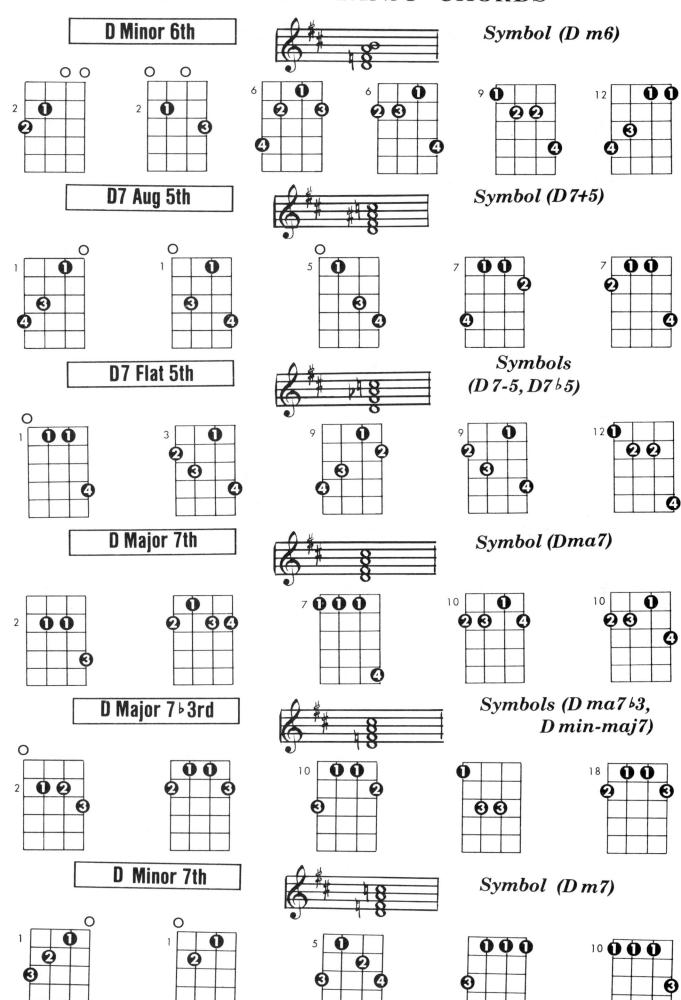

BLUEGRASS BANJO CHORDS

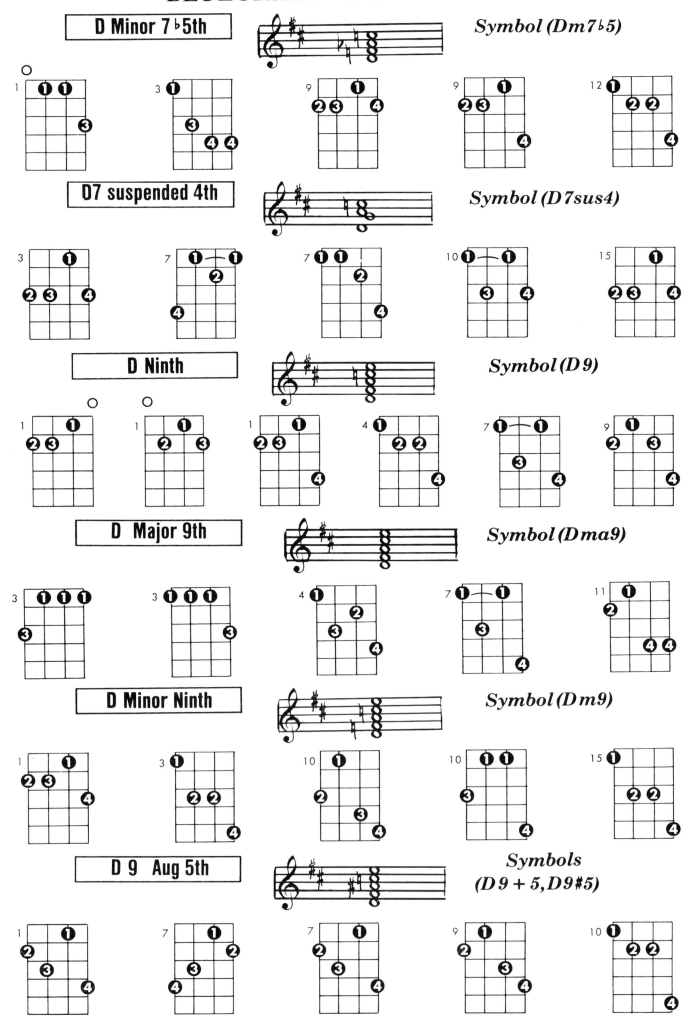

D Minor 7 ♭5th   *Symbol (Dm7♭5)*

D7 suspended 4th   *Symbol (D7sus4)*

D Ninth   *Symbol (D9)*

D Major 9th   *Symbol (Dma9)*

D Minor Ninth   *Symbol (Dm9)*

D 9 Aug 5th   *Symbols (D9 + 5, D9#5)*

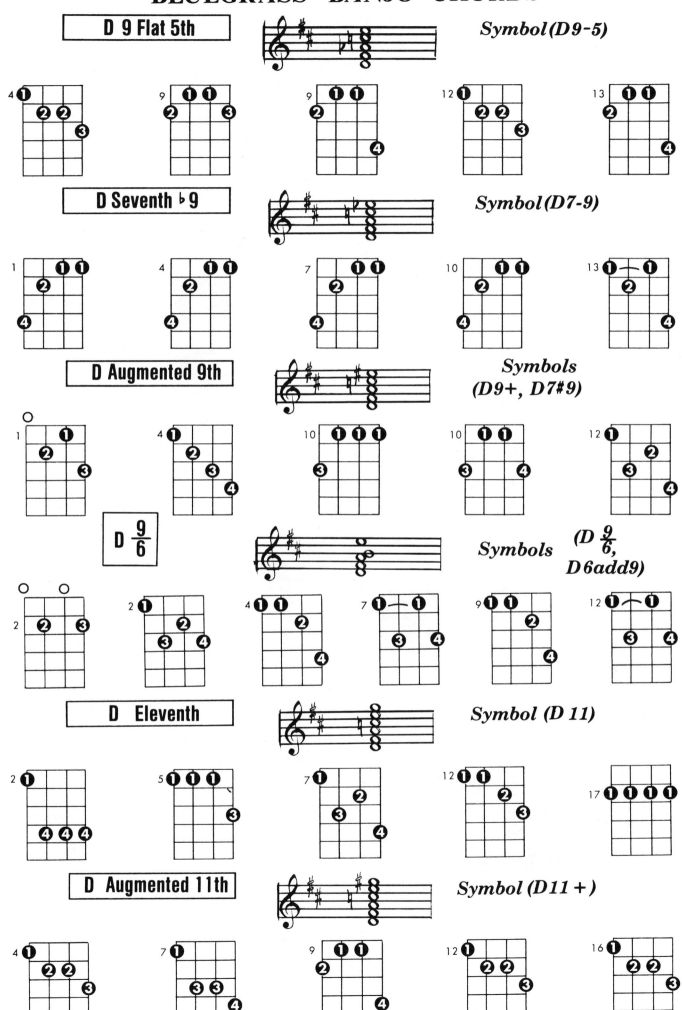

BLUEGRASS BANJO CHORDS

D Thirteenth

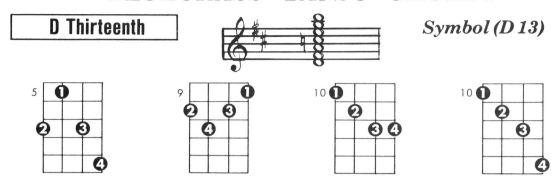

Symbol (D 13)

BLUEGRASS BANJO CHORDS

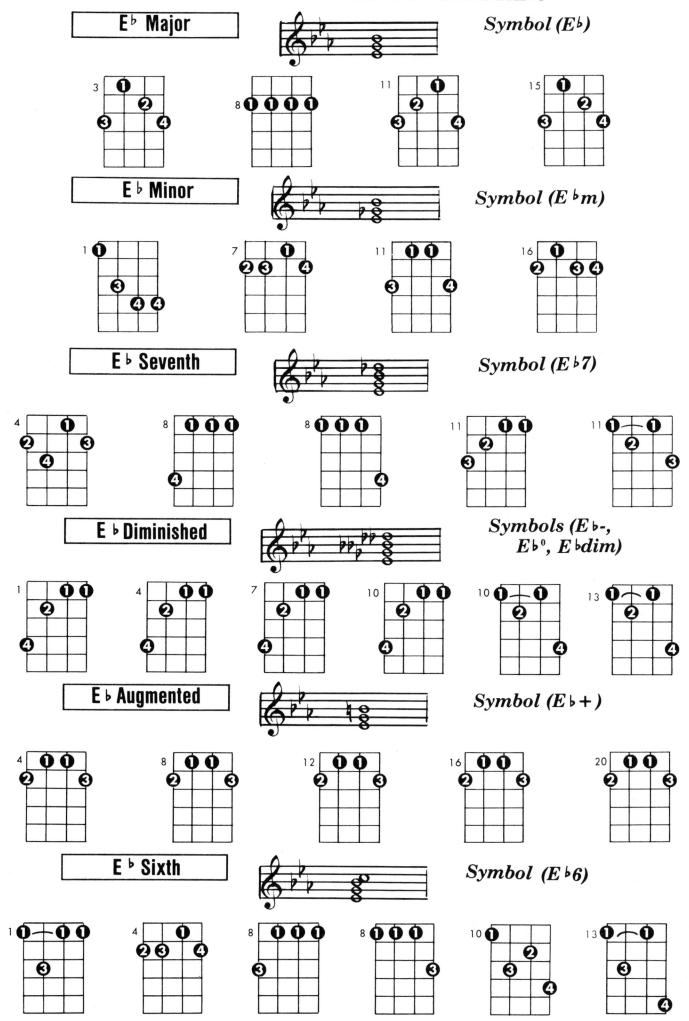

BLUEGRASS BANJO CHORDS

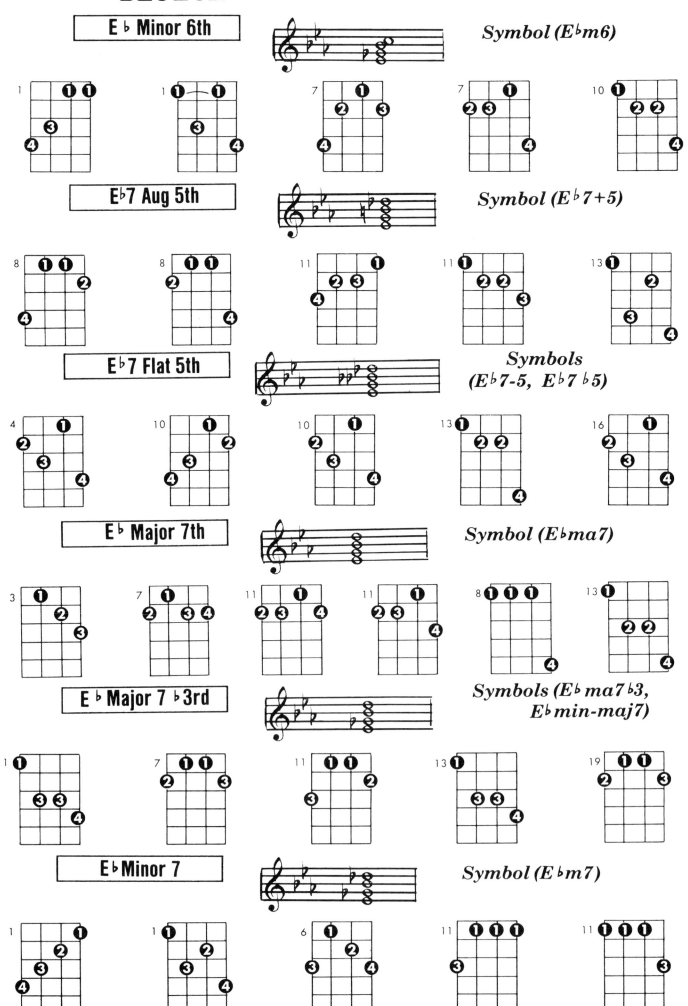

BLUEGRASS BANJO CHORDS

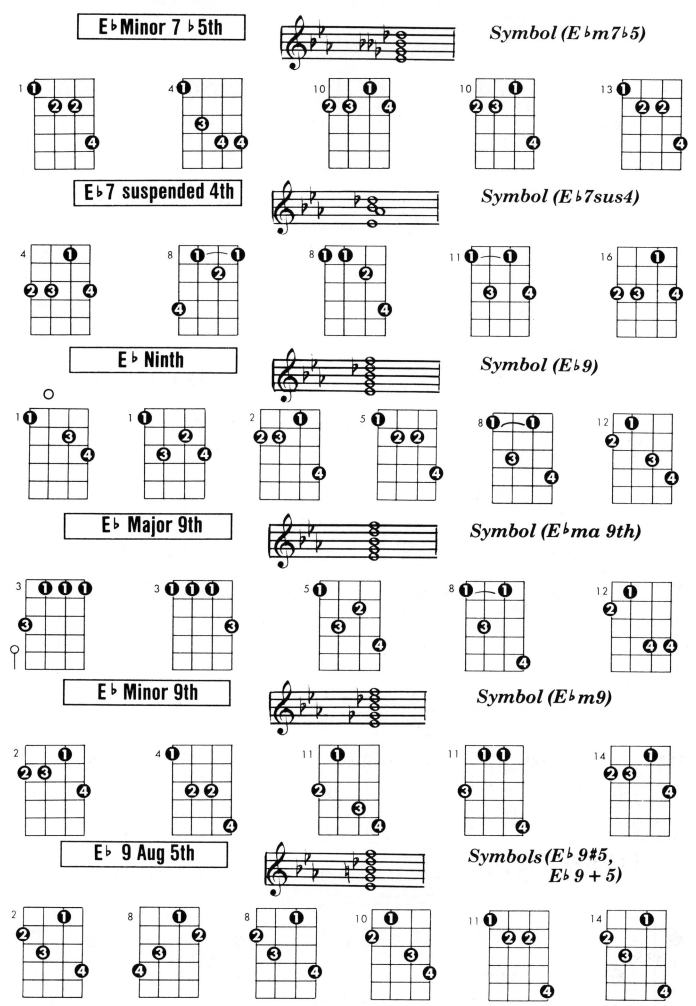

Eb Minor 7 b5th — Symbol (Eb m7b5)

Eb7 suspended 4th — Symbol (Eb7sus4)

Eb Ninth — Symbol (Eb9)

Eb Major 9th — Symbol (Ebma 9th)

Eb Minor 9th — Symbol (Ebm9)

Eb 9 Aug 5th — Symbols (Eb9#5, Eb9+5)

BLUEGRASS BANJO CHORDS

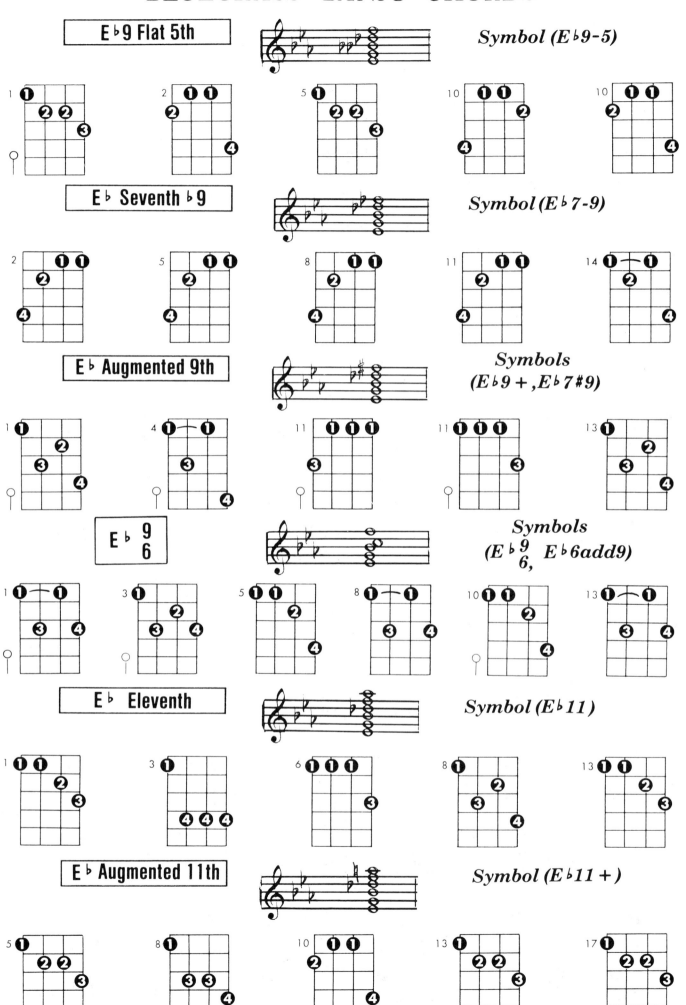

E♭ Thirteenth

Symbol (E♭13)

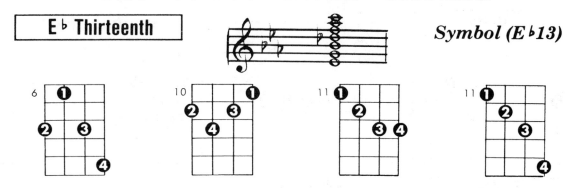

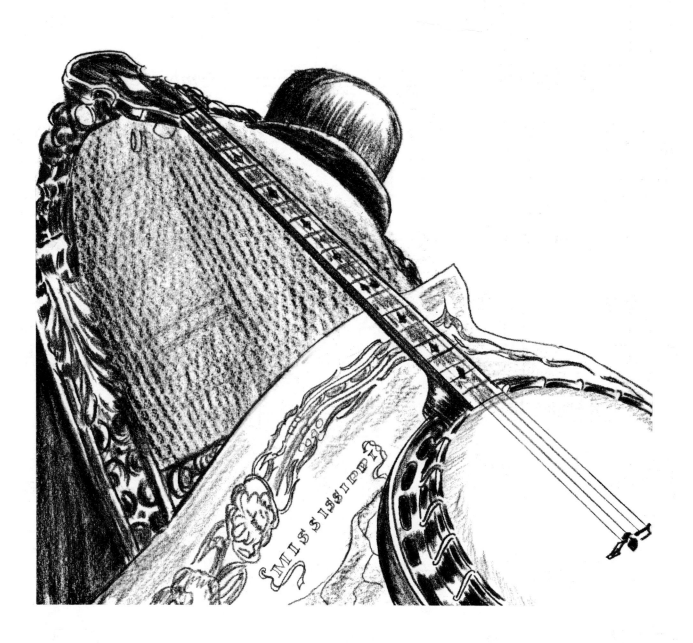

BLUEGRASS BANJO CHORDS

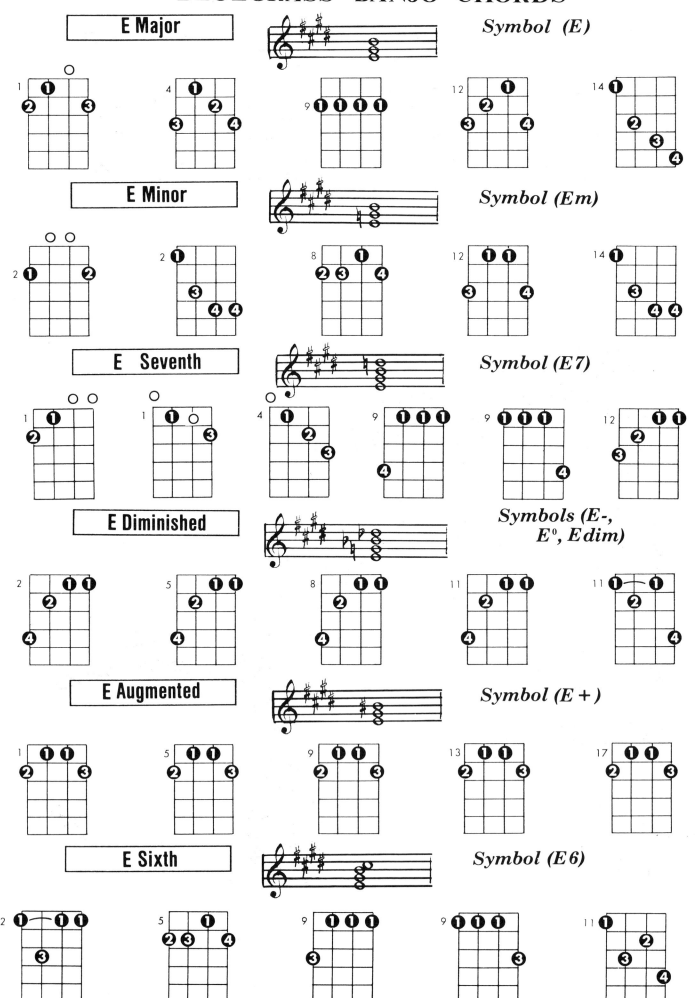

E Major — Symbol (E)

E Minor — Symbol (Em)

E Seventh — Symbol (E7)

E Diminished — Symbols (E-, E⁰, Edim)

E Augmented — Symbol (E+)

E Sixth — Symbol (E6)

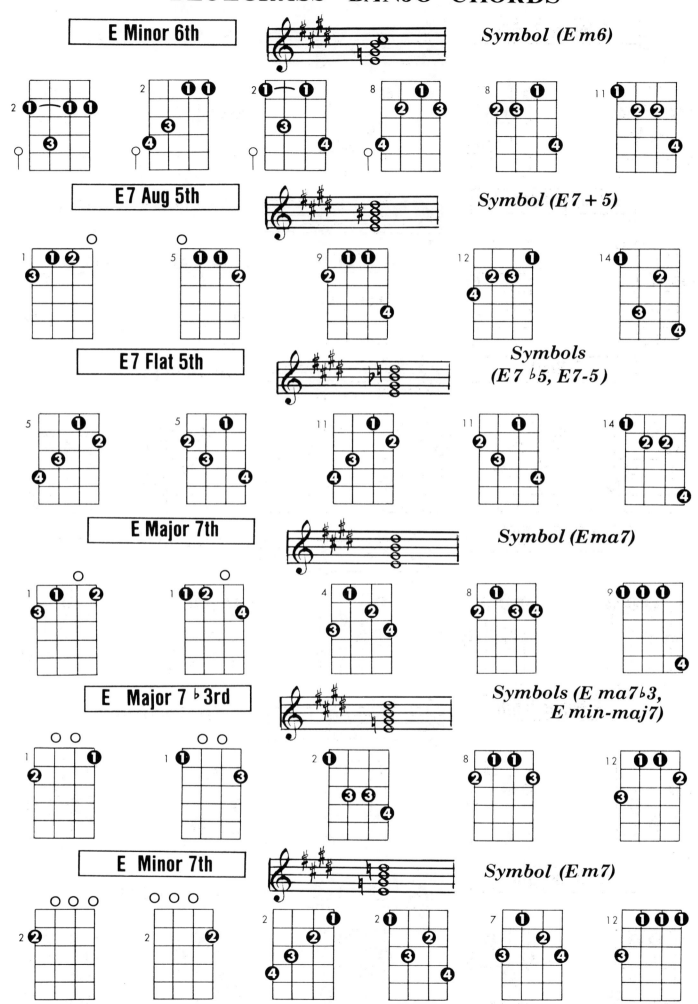

BLUEGRASS BANJO CHORDS

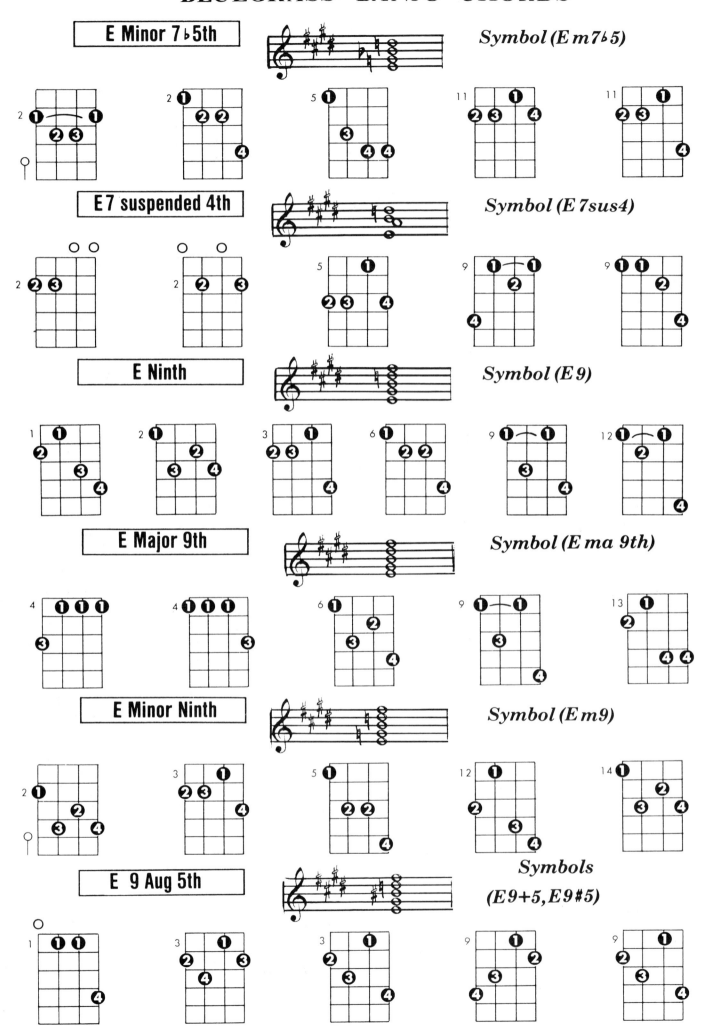

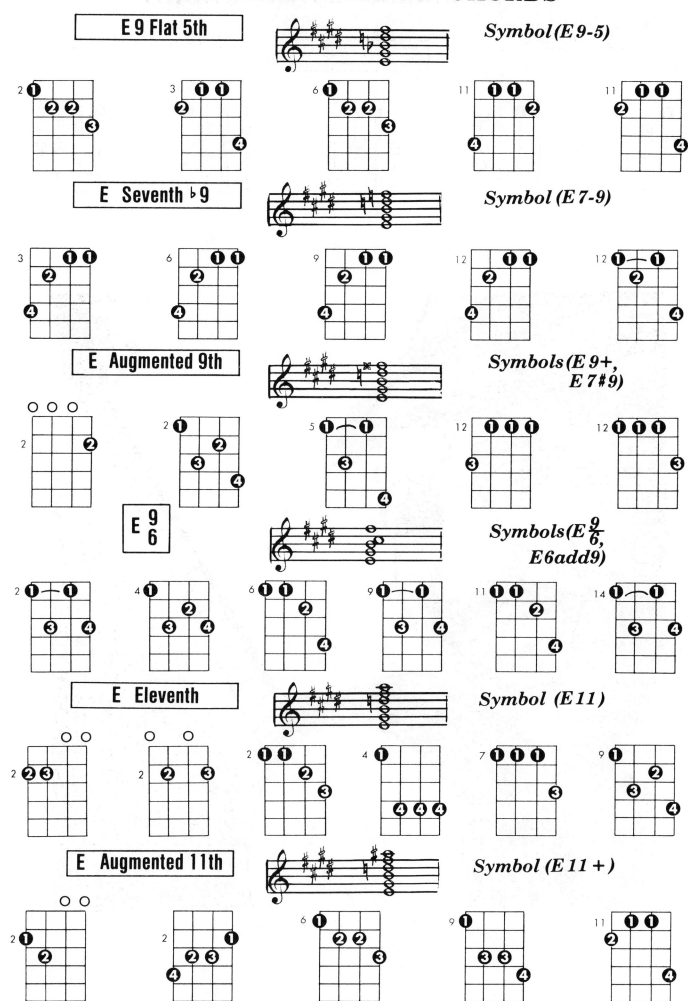

BLUEGRASS BANJO CHORDS

E Thirteenth

Symbol (E 13)

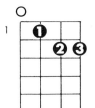
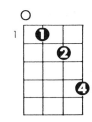
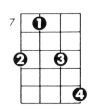
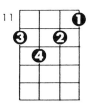
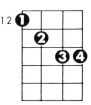

BLUEGRASS BANJO CHORDS

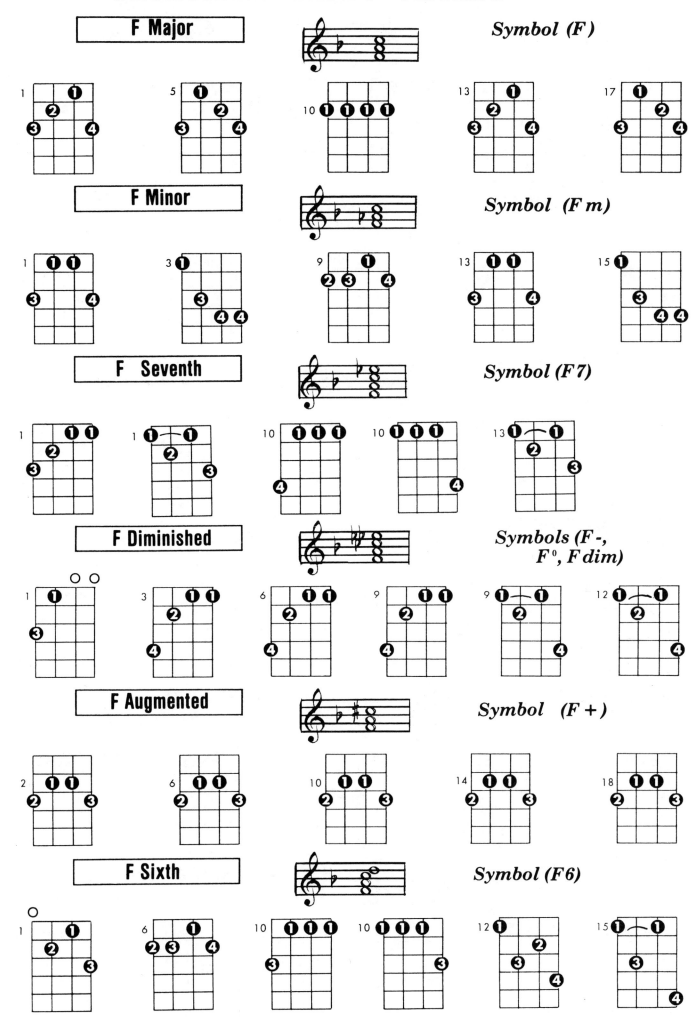

BLUEGRASS BANJO CHORDS

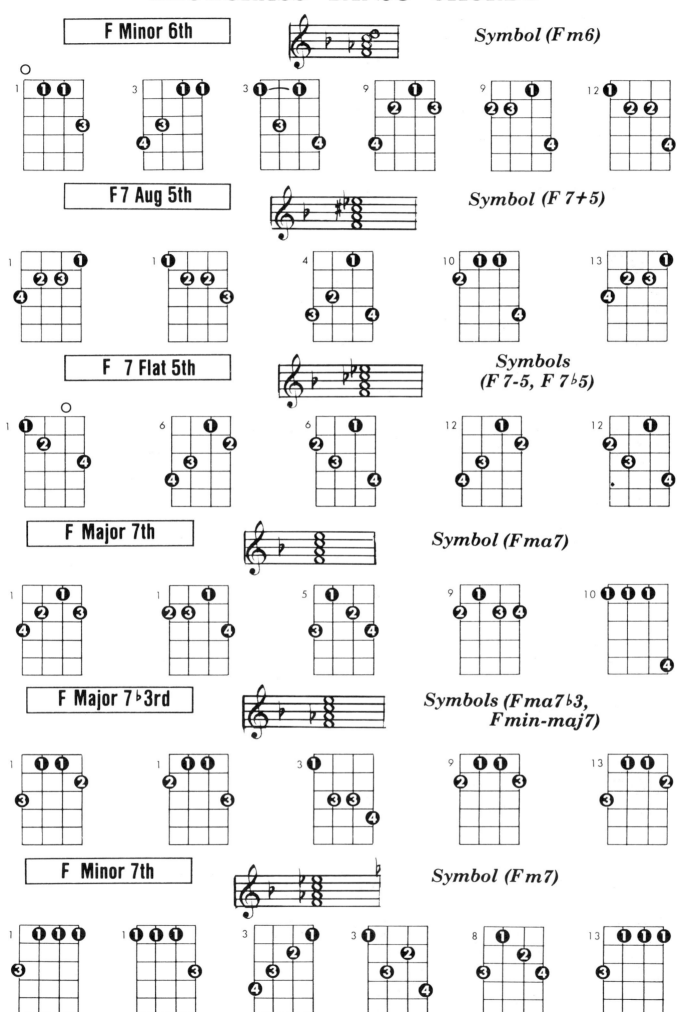

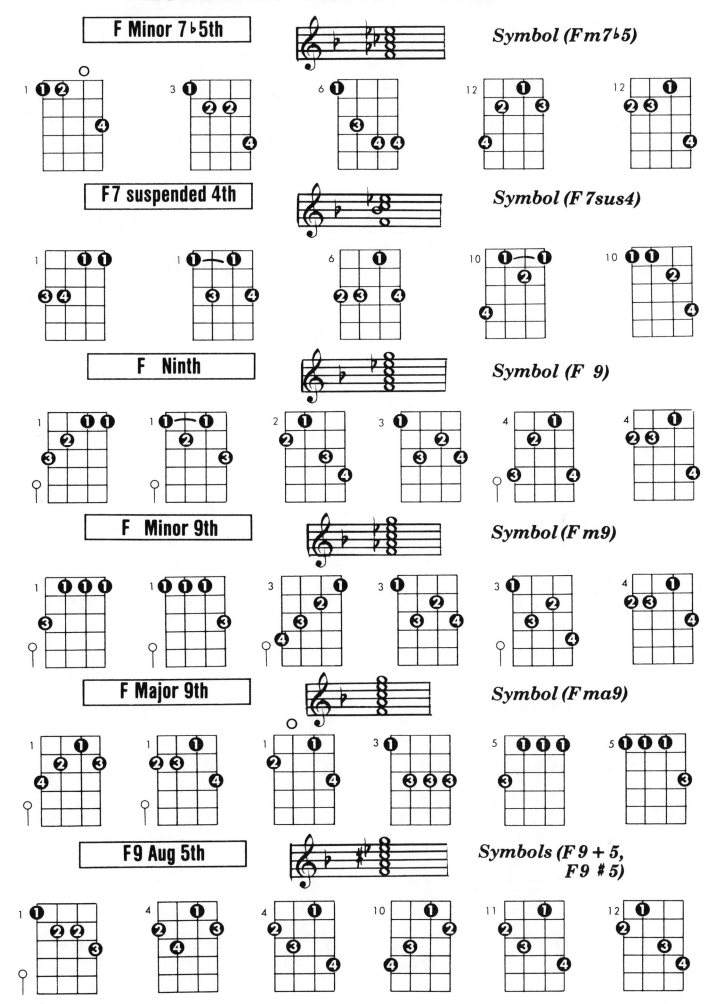

BLUEGRASS BANJO CHORDS

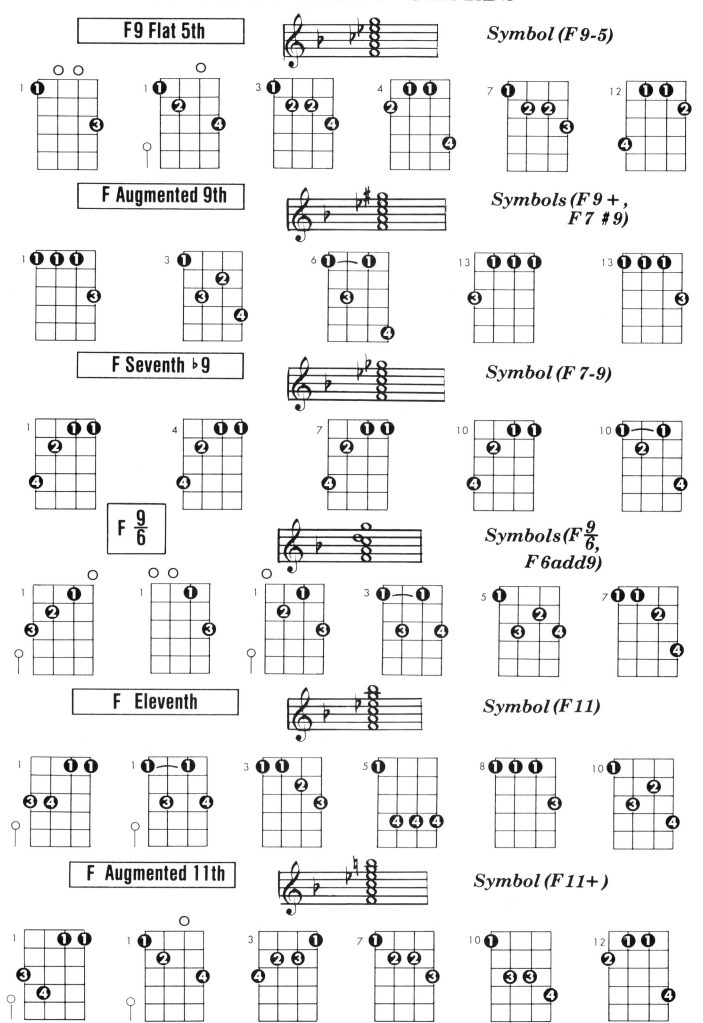

F9 Flat 5th — *Symbol (F 9-5)*

F Augmented 9th — *Symbols (F 9+, F 7 #9)*

F Seventh ♭9 — *Symbol (F 7-9)*

F 9/6 — *Symbols (F 9/6, F 6add9)*

F Eleventh — *Symbol (F 11)*

F Augmented 11th — *Symbol (F 11+)*

F Thirteenth

Symbol (F 13)

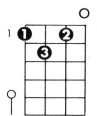
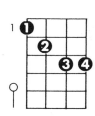
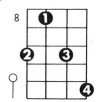
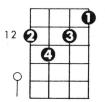
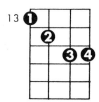

BLUEGRASS BANJO CHORDS

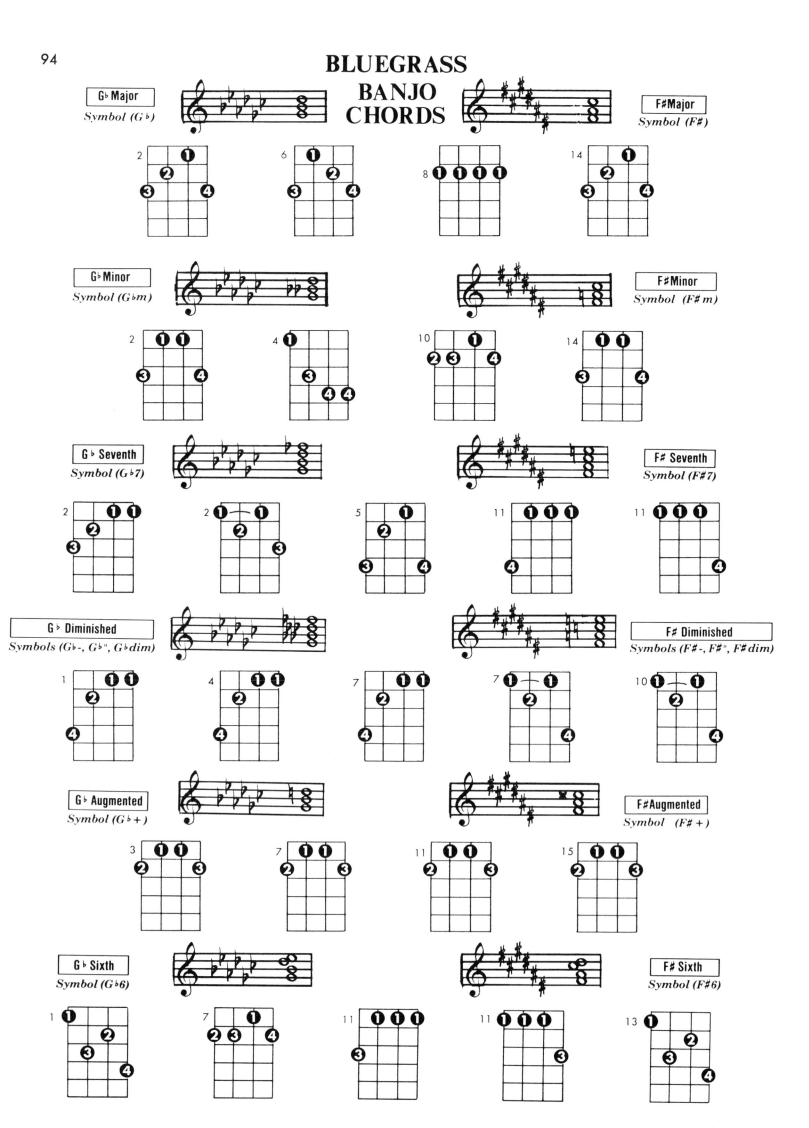

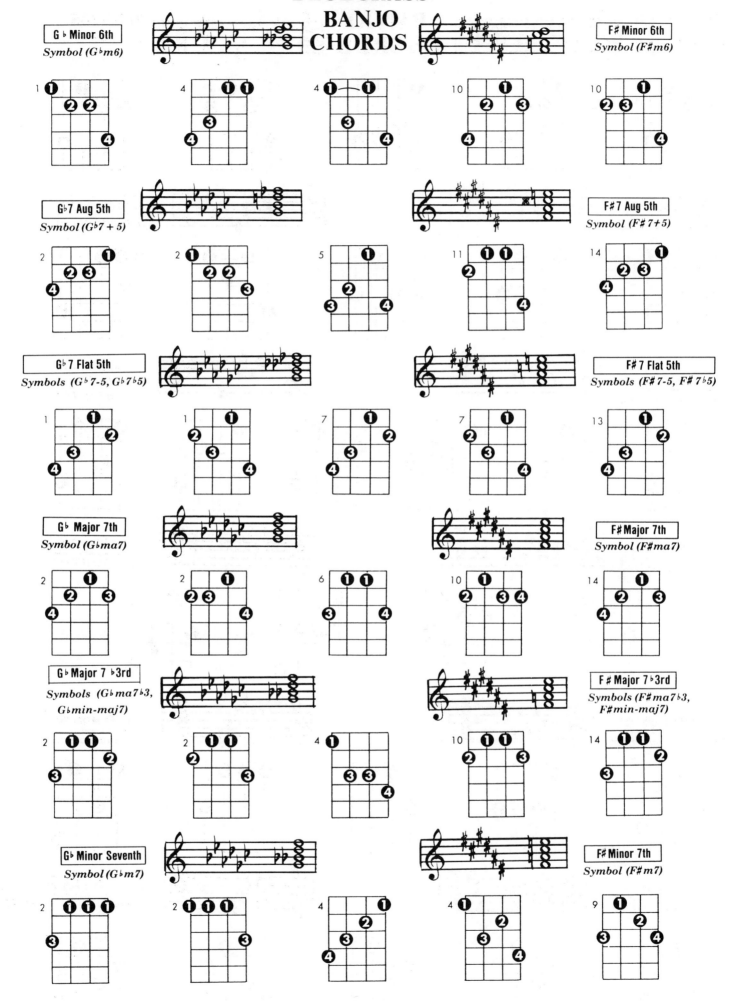

BLUEGRASS BANJO CHORDS

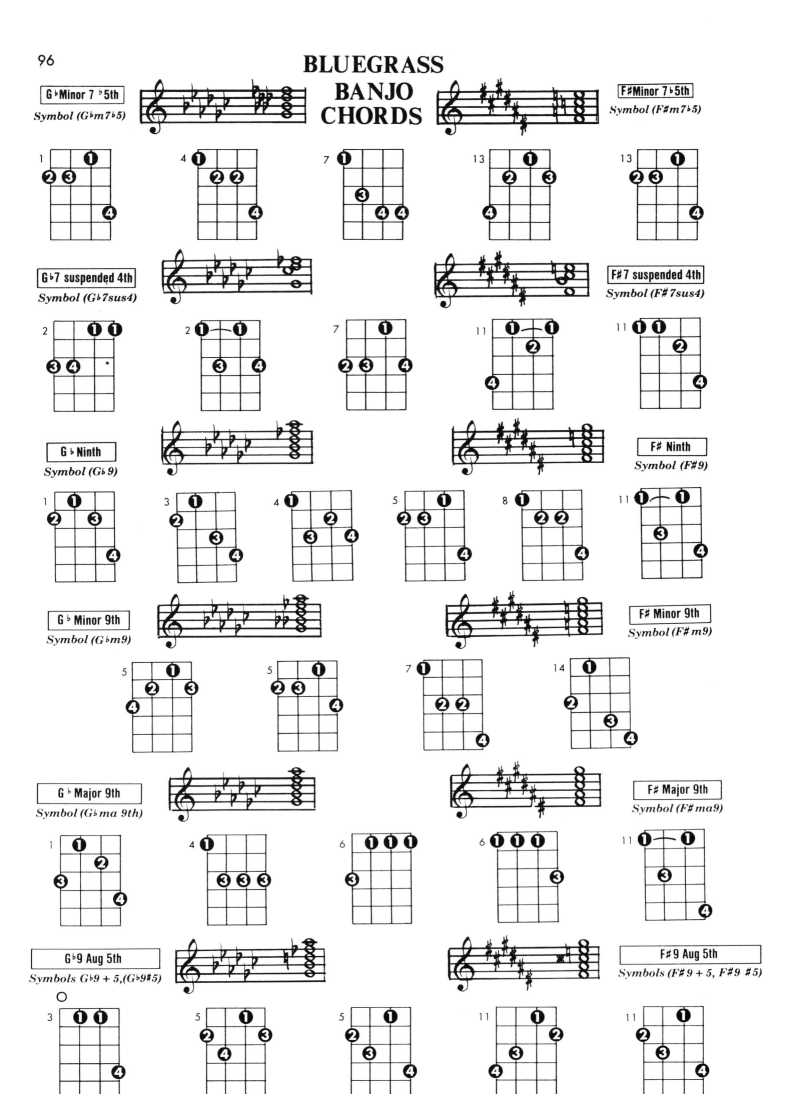

BLUEGRASS BANJO CHORDS

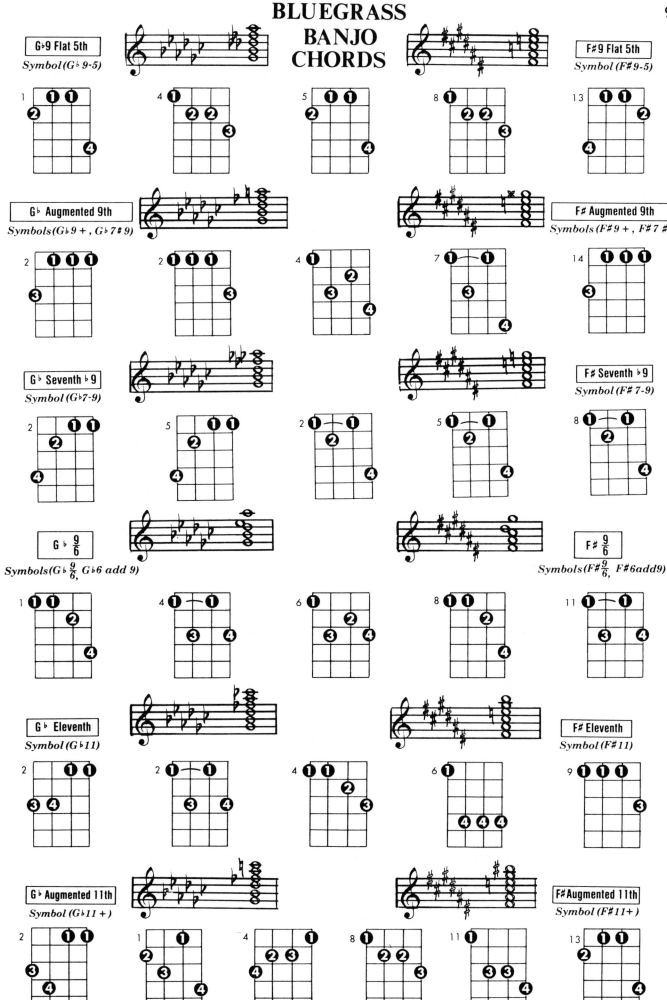

BLUEGRASS BANJO CHORDS

G♭ Thirteenth
Symbol (G♭13)

F♯ Thirteenth
Symbol (F♯13)

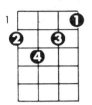

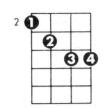

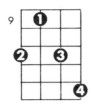

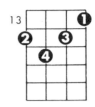

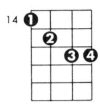

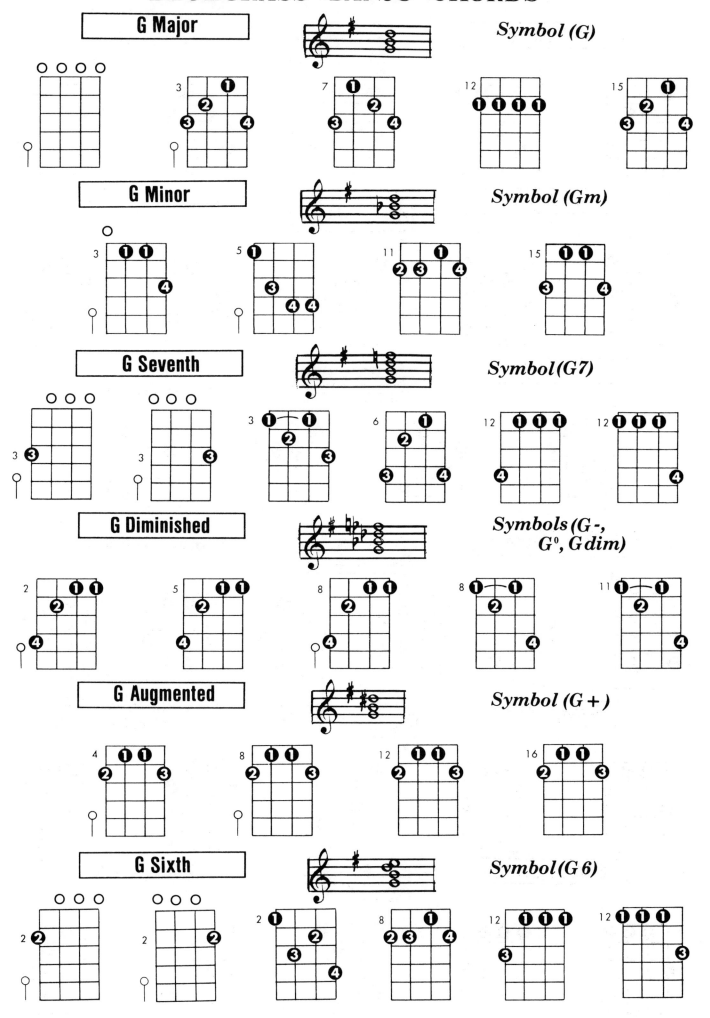

BLUEGRASS BANJO CHORDS

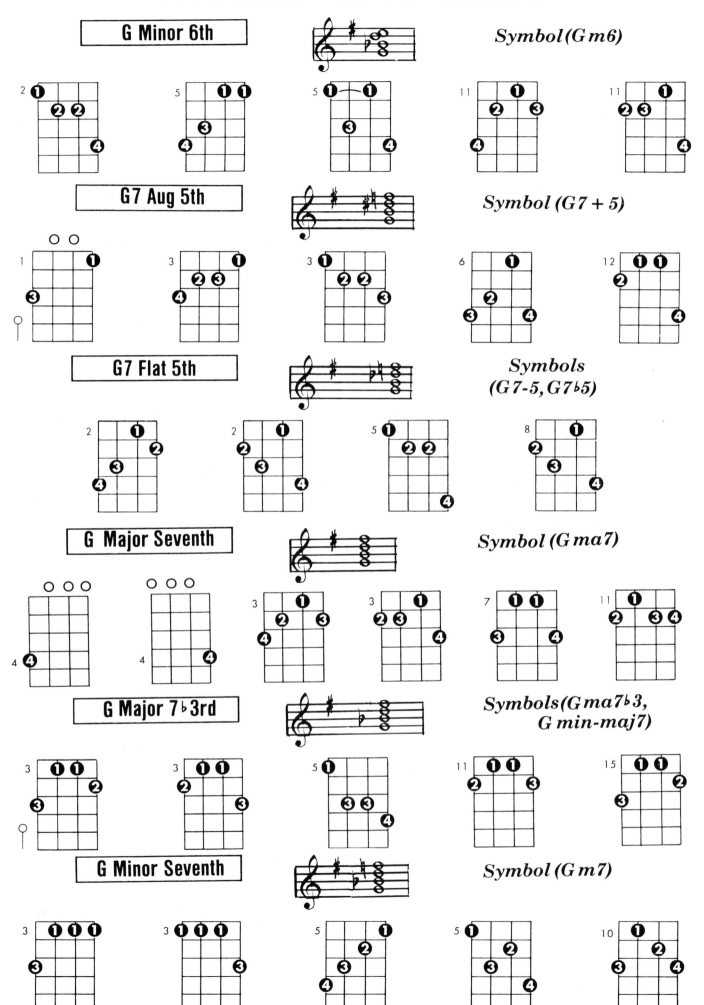

G Minor 6th — *Symbol (G m6)*

G7 Aug 5th — *Symbol (G7 + 5)*

G7 Flat 5th — *Symbols (G7-5, G7♭5)*

G Major Seventh — *Symbol (G ma7)*

G Major 7♭3rd — *Symbols (G ma7♭3, G min-maj7)*

G Minor Seventh — *Symbol (G m7)*

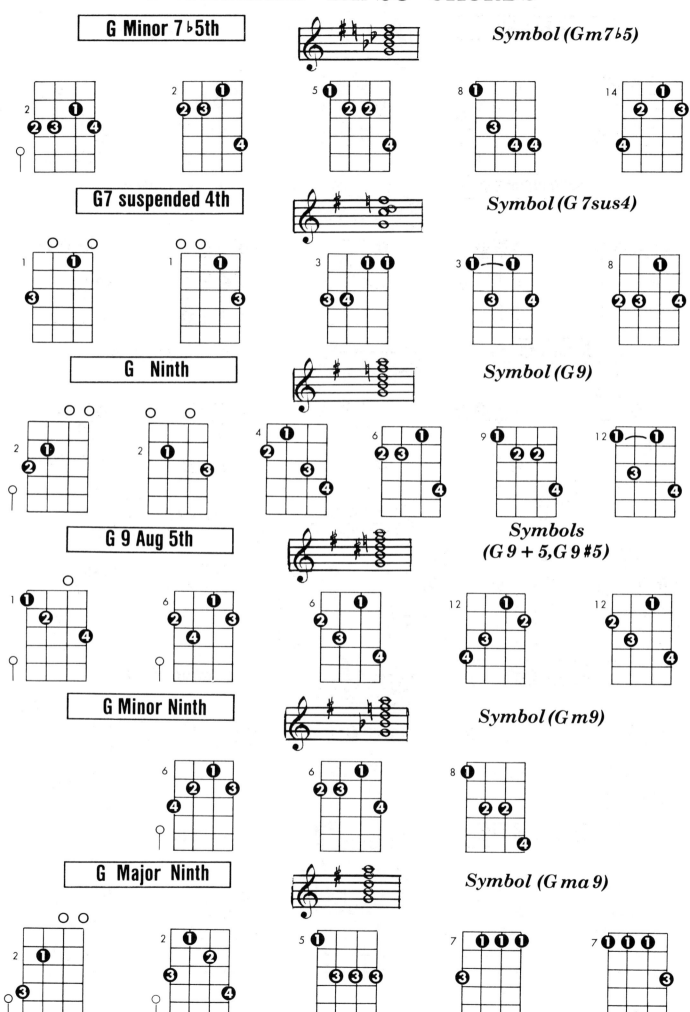

BLUEGRASS BANJO CHORDS

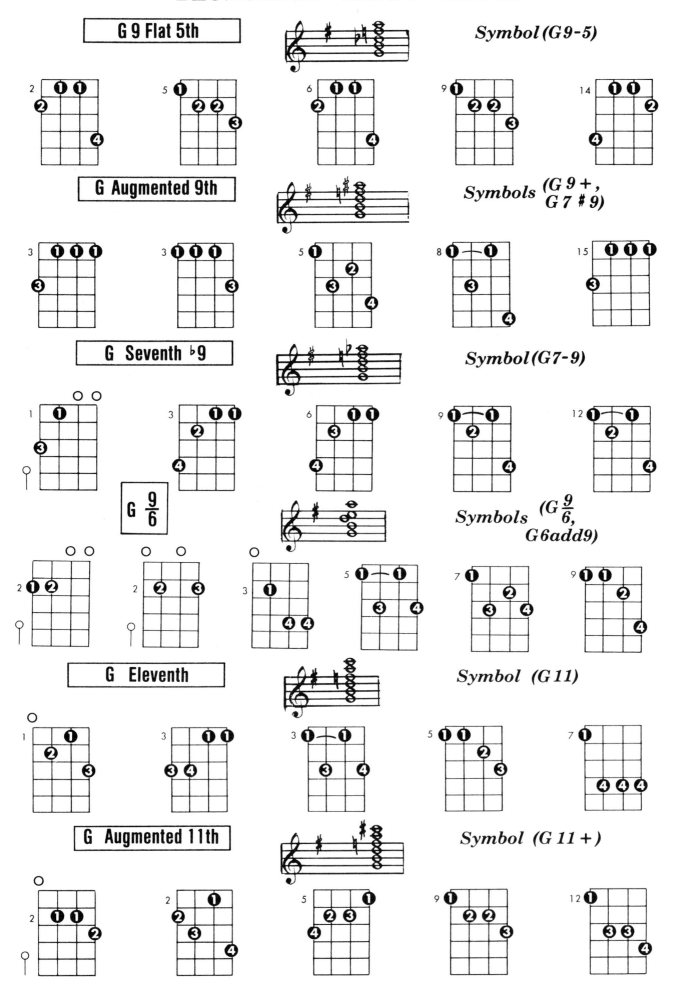

G 9 Flat 5th

Symbol (G9-5)

G Augmented 9th

Symbols (G 9 +, G 7 ♯ 9)

G Seventh ♭9

Symbol (G7-9)

G 9/6

Symbols (G 9/6, G6add9)

G Eleventh

Symbol (G 11)

G Augmented 11th

Symbol (G 11 +)

G Thirteenth

Symbol (G 13)

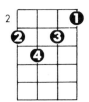
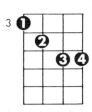

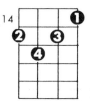
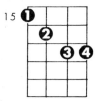

BLUEGRASS BANJO CHORDS

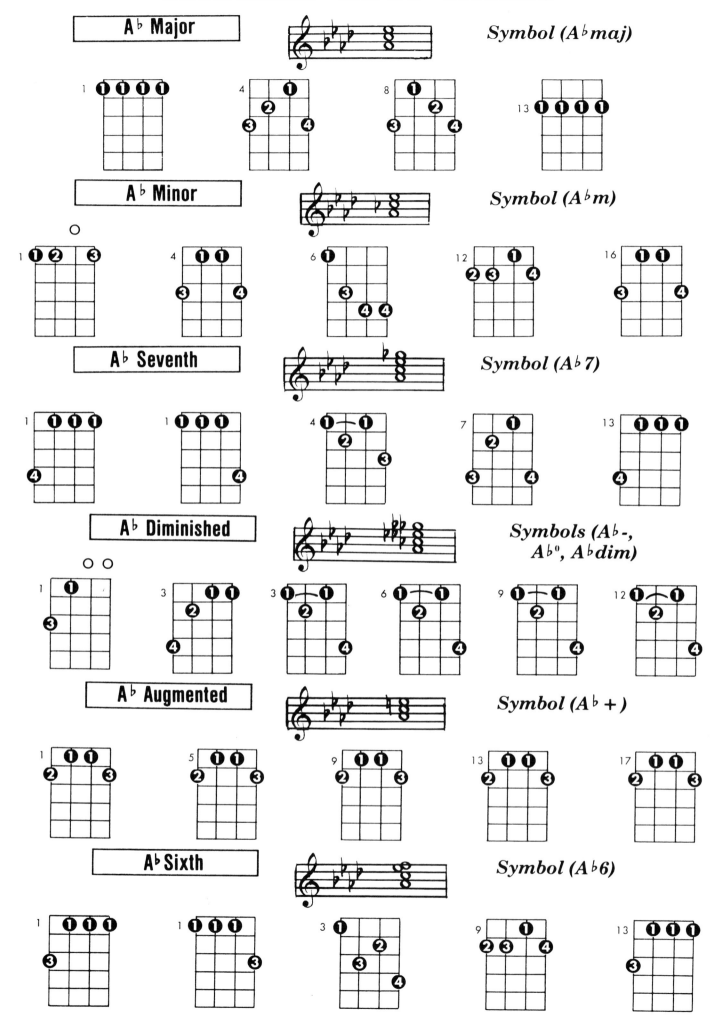

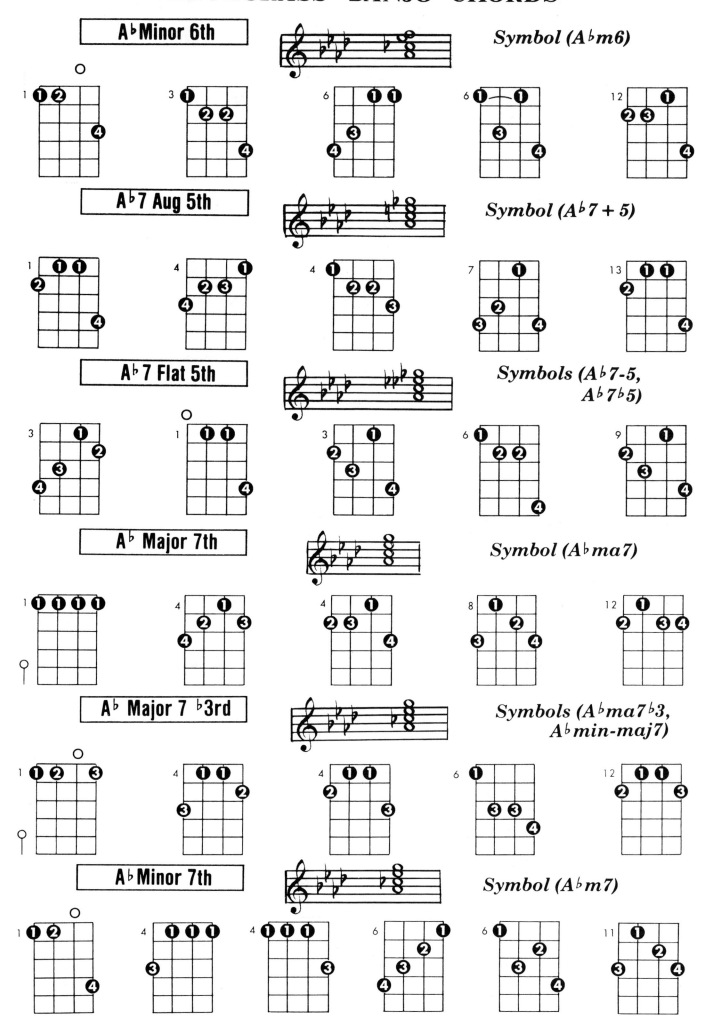

BLUEGRASS BANJO CHORDS

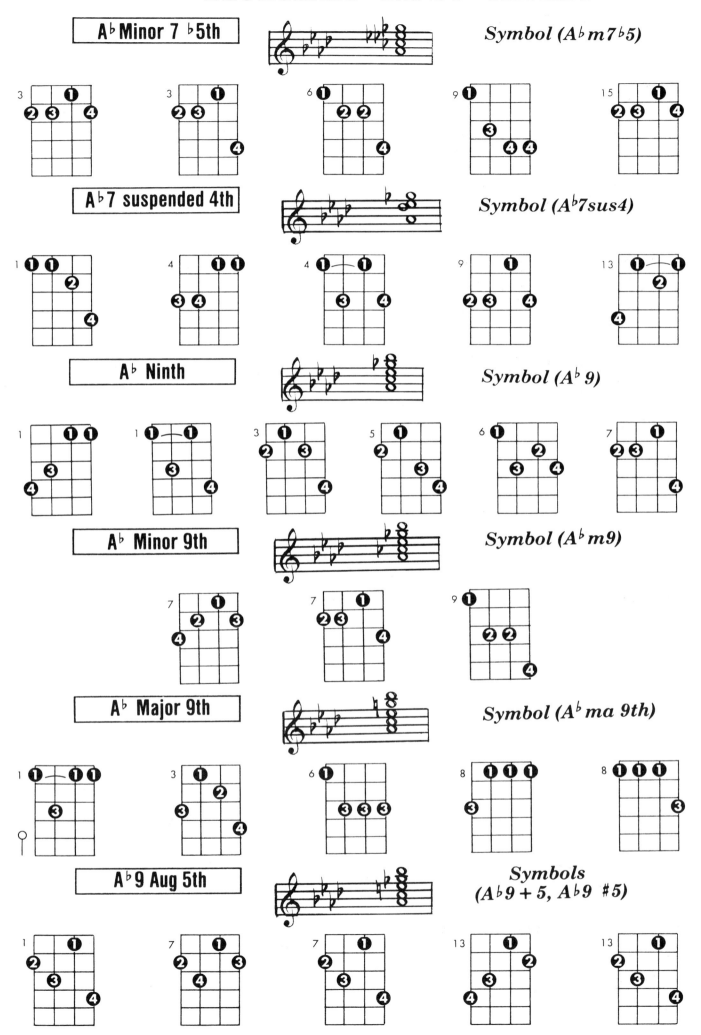

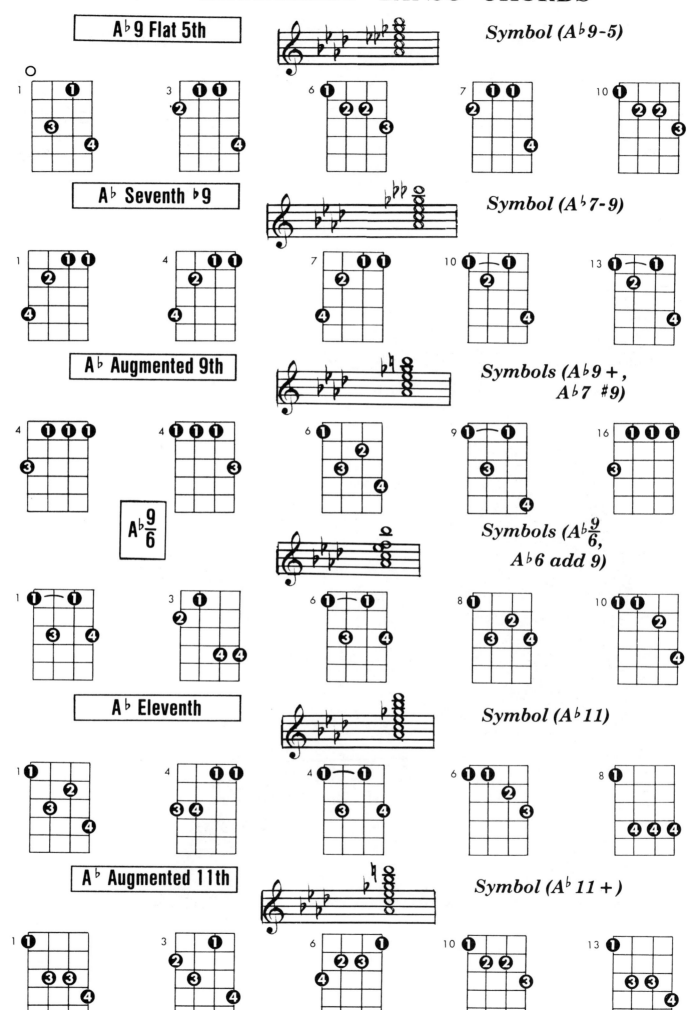

BLUEGRASS BANJO CHORDS

A♭ Thirteenth

Symbol (A♭13)

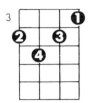

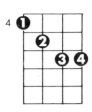

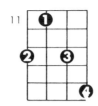

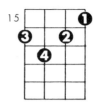

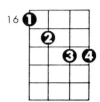

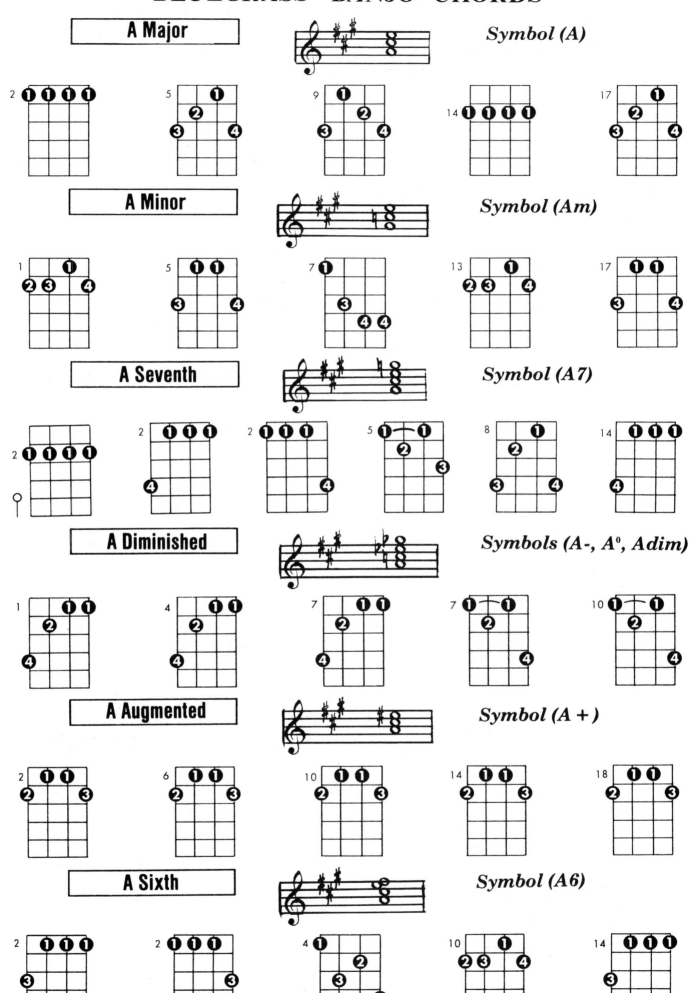

BLUEGRASS BANJO CHORDS

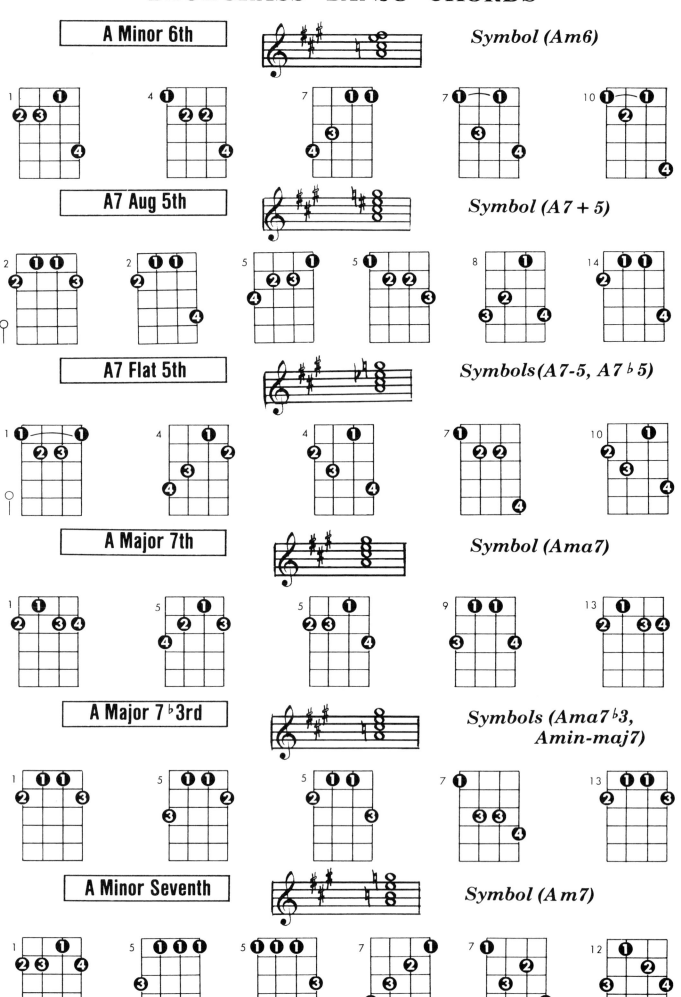

A Minor 6th — Symbol (Am6)

A7 Aug 5th — Symbol (A7 + 5)

A7 Flat 5th — Symbols (A7-5, A7♭5)

A Major 7th — Symbol (Ama7)

A Major 7♭3rd — Symbols (Ama7♭3, Amin-maj7)

A Minor Seventh — Symbol (Am7)

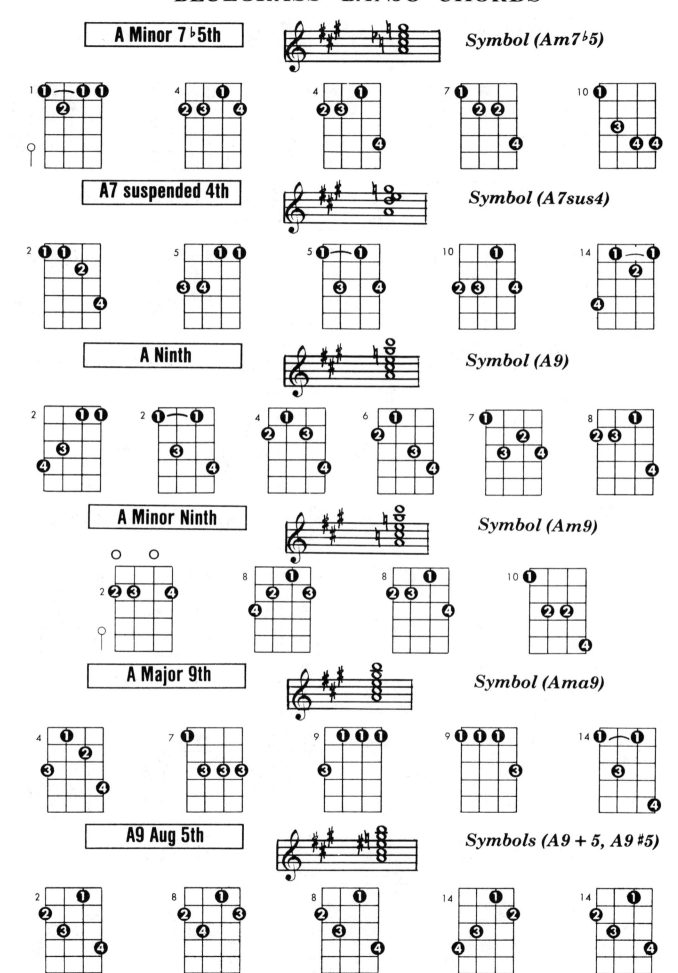

BLUEGRASS BANJO CHORDS

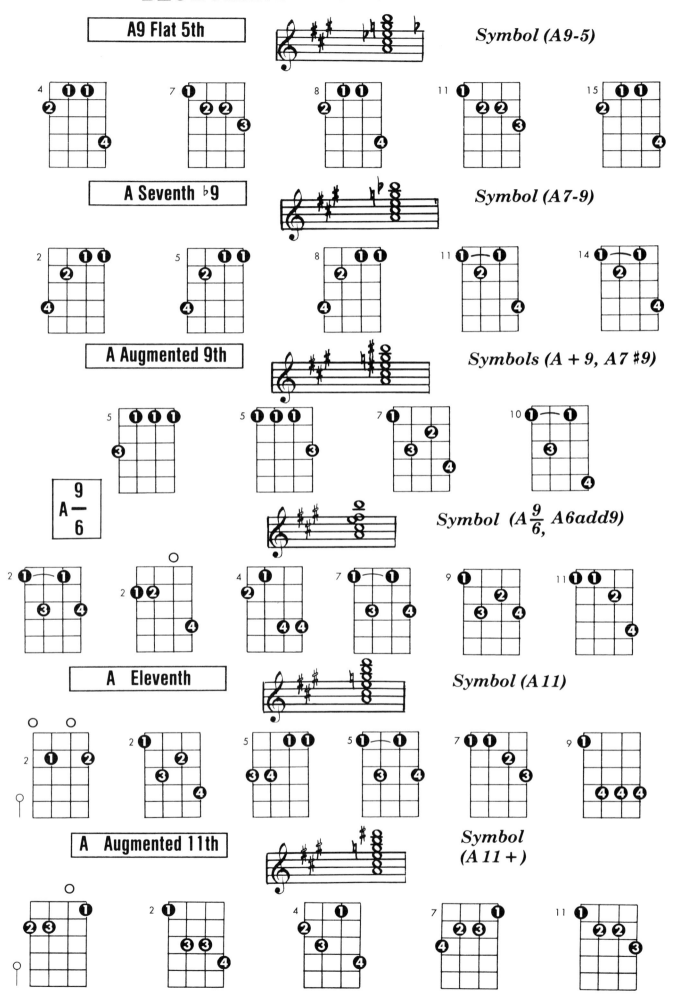

BLUEGRASS BANJO CHORDS

A Thirteenth

Symbol (A 13)

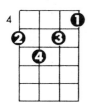
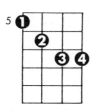
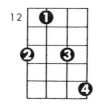

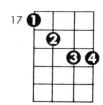

BLUEGRASS BANJO CHORDS

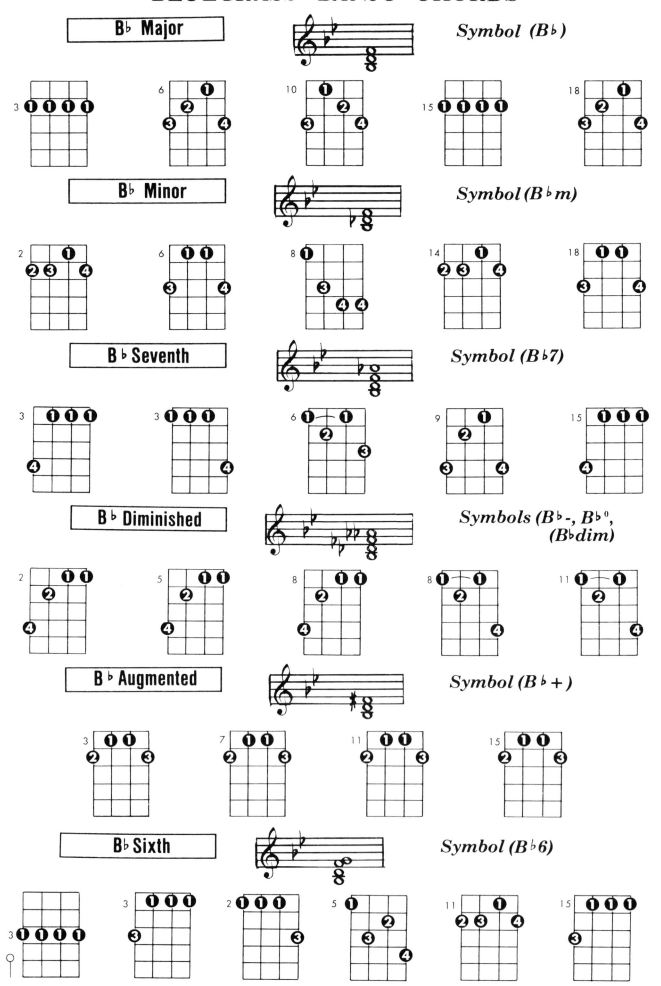

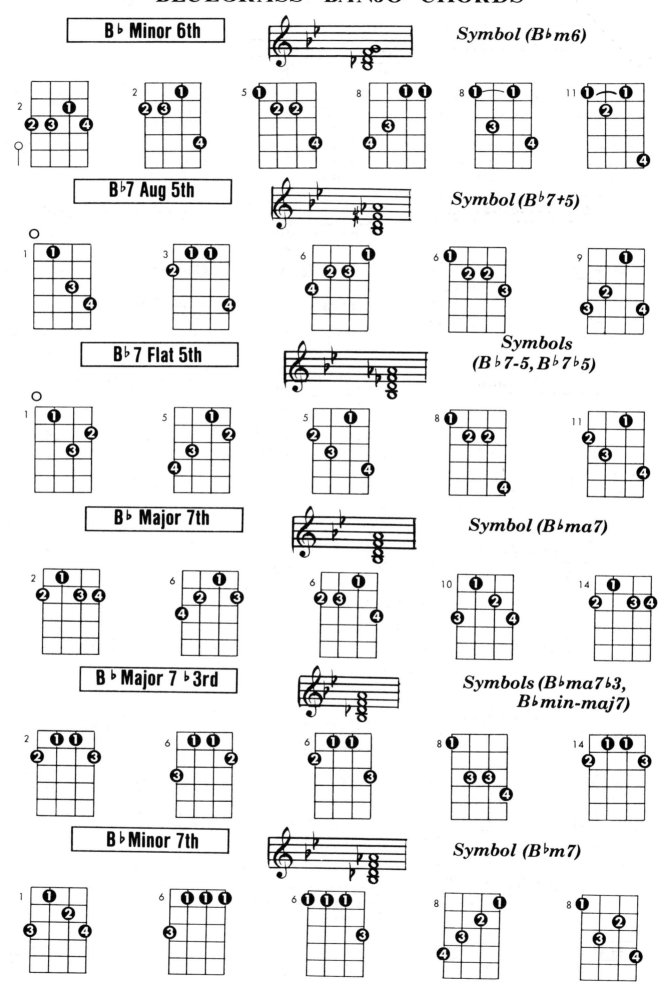

BLUEGRASS BANJO CHORDS

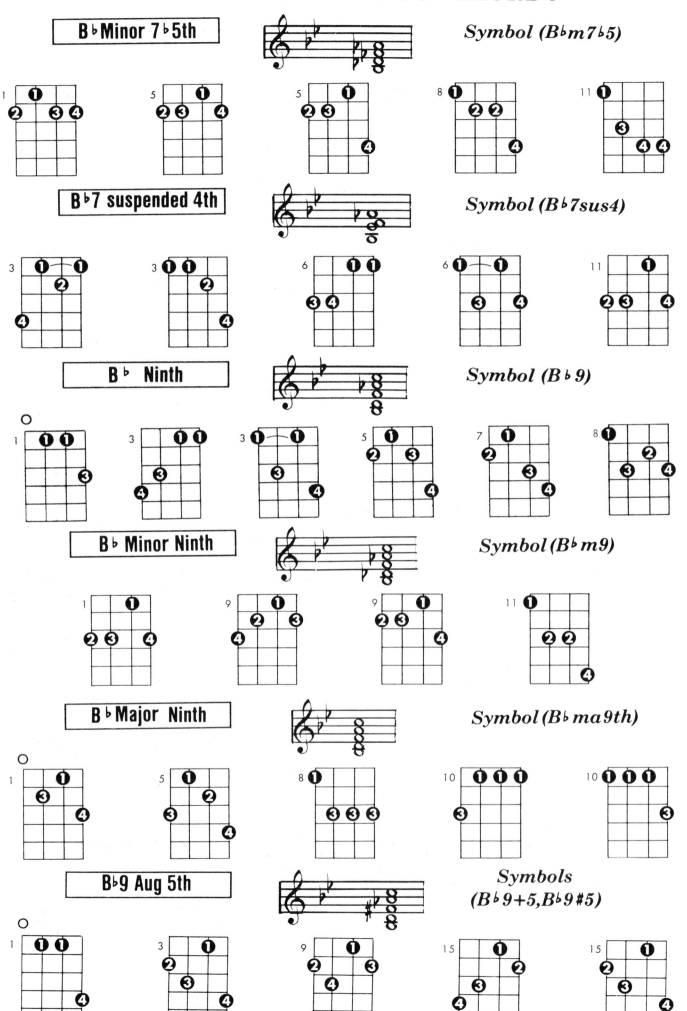

B♭ Minor 7♭5th — Symbol (B♭m7♭5)

B♭7 suspended 4th — Symbol (B♭7sus4)

B♭ Ninth — Symbol (B♭9)

B♭ Minor Ninth — Symbol (B♭m9)

B♭ Major Ninth — Symbol (B♭ma9th)

B♭9 Aug 5th — Symbols (B♭9+5, B♭9#5)

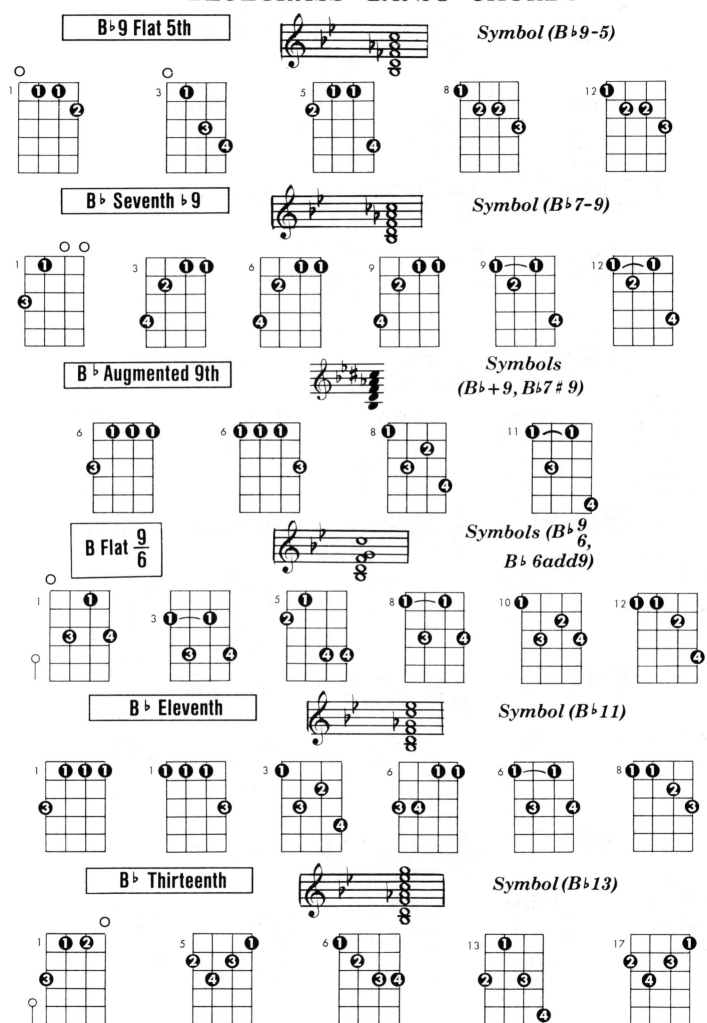

BLUEGRASS BANJO CHORDS

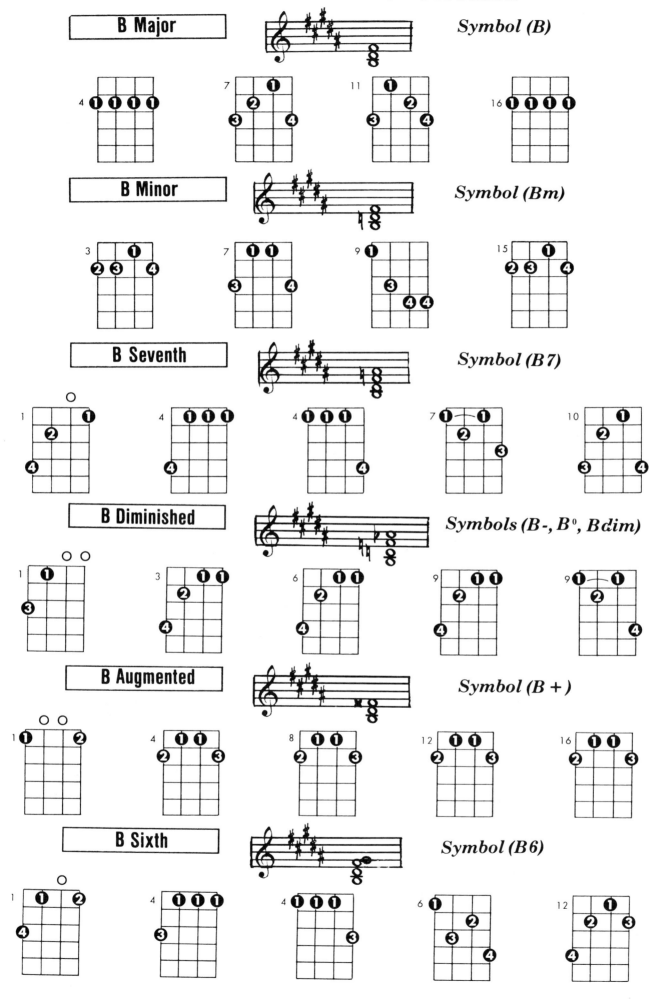

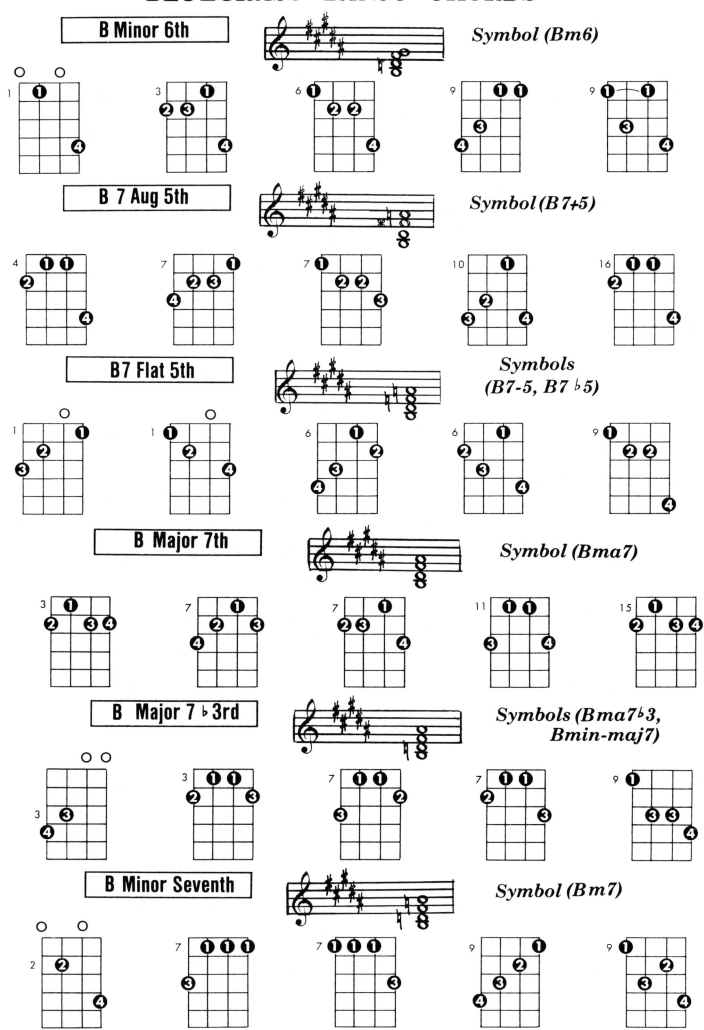

BLUEGRASS BANJO CHORDS

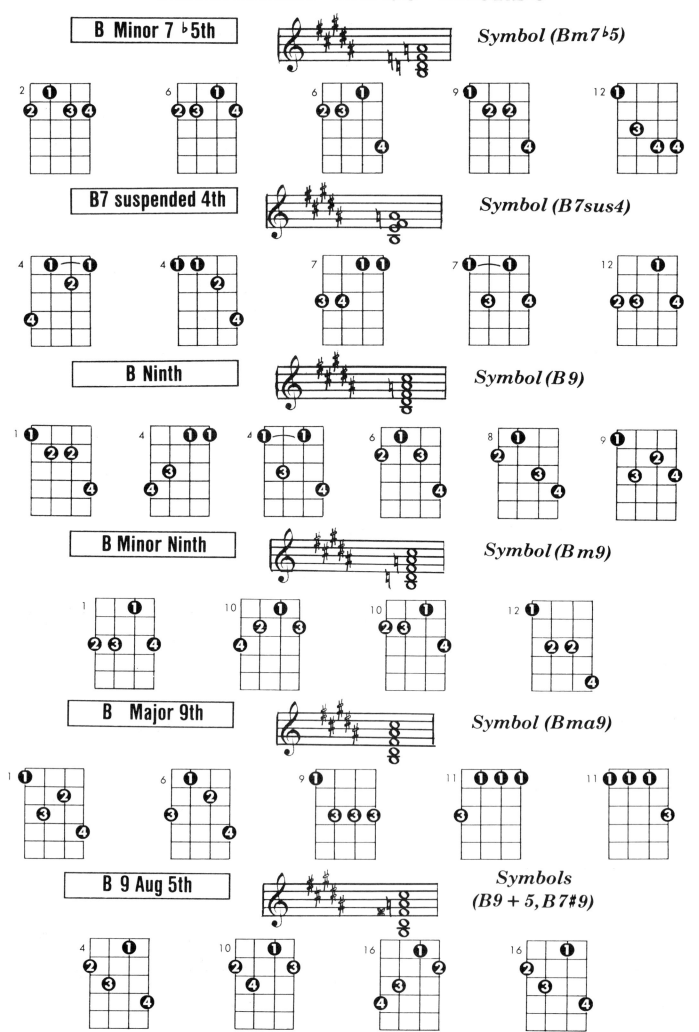

BLUEGRASS BANJO CHORDS

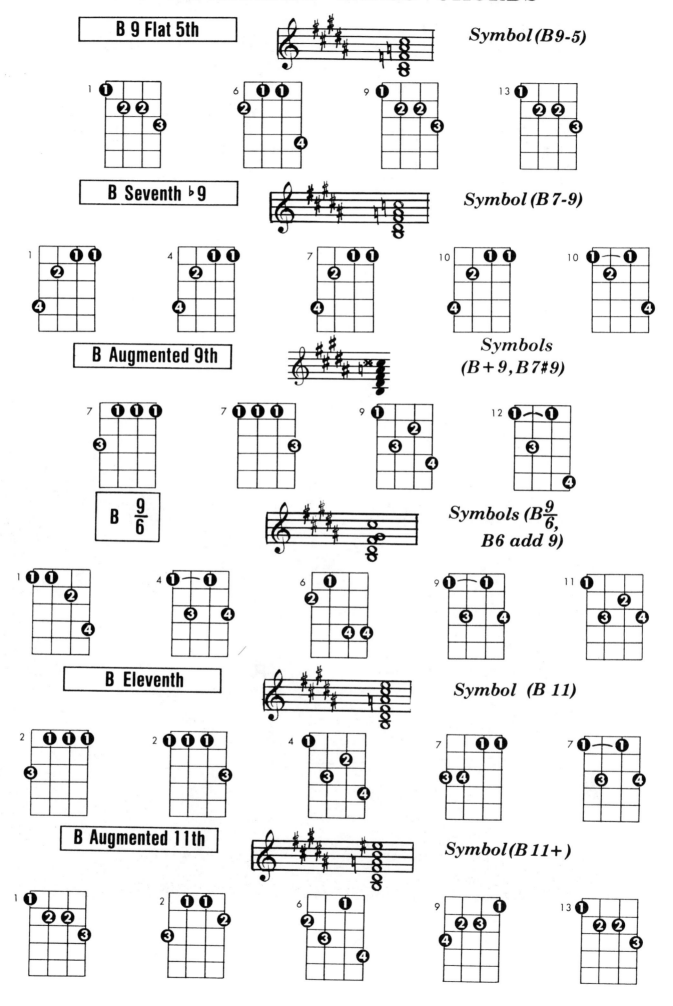

BLUEGRASS BANJO CHORDS

B Thirteenth

Symbol (B 13)

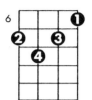 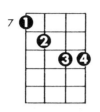 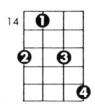 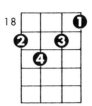

The Correct Way To Hold The Banjo

This Is the Pick

Hold it in

this manner ———————→

firmly between the

thumb and first finger.

Use a medium

soft pick.

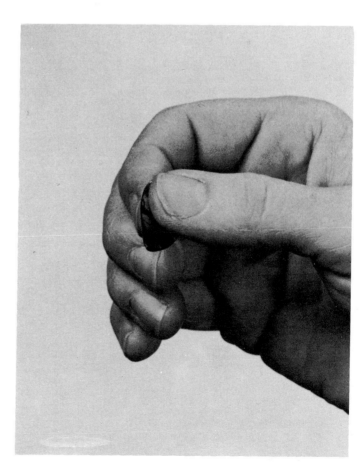

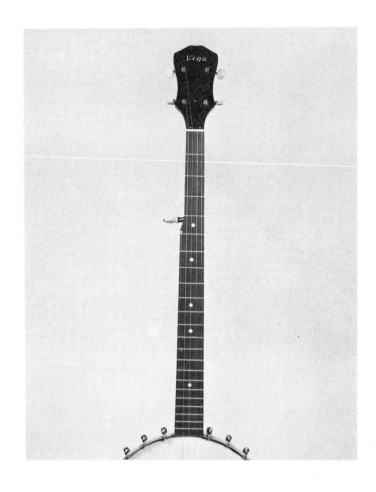

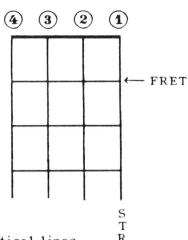

The vertical lines
are the strings.

The horizontal lines
are the frets.

The encircled numbers
are the number of the strings.

= 5th String
(open)

Striking the Strings

with the fingers

with the pick

THE RIGHT HAND

RIGHT HAND POSITION

The right hand is by far the most important thing in playing Banjo, Bluegrass Style.

The ring finger and little finger are placed in a stationary position, near the bridge, and should remain in this position at all times. The wrist can be bent to give maximum power in your roll.

The hand should be placed in a comfortable position while playing. Yet, it is also important to your playing to have it in the best position to obtain the best tone from your instrument.

USE OF THUMB AND FINGERS

The middle finger (designated in the tunes by a 2) is always used <u>only</u> on the first string.

The index finger (designated by the number 1) is used on the second and third strings <u>only</u>.

The thumb (designated by letter T) is used on the second, third, fourth and fifth strings.

PICKS

For best tone quality, I suggest metal picks for the index and middle fingers and a plastic thumb pick. These can be purchased at any music store where parts or supplies for instruments are sold.

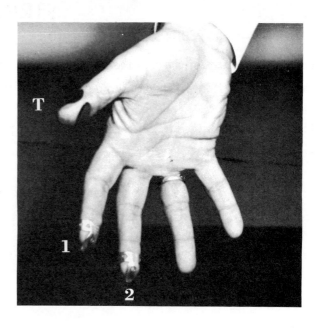

BRIDGE

The 'ring' or sound of a banjo can be altered in several ways.

If the sound is too deep or coarse, use a higher bridge. Also, tighten the head until it is firm.

You can also thin that part of the bridge where the strings cross over it. Use a very fine file or light sandpaper. The thinner the bridge, the brighter the sound.

When you have your banjo set up to give its best tone, consistently and to your satisfaction — it's a good idea not to allow many people to play it or work on it. Everyone has his own idea on how a banjo should sound, and a fairly strong "Hands off" policy can save you a lot of trouble.

ADJUSTING THE BRIDGE

If ever your banjo does not note true from the 12th to the 22nd fret, you can correct this by adjusting the bridge.

If the banjo notes flat, move the bridge forward, toward the neck to the desired position.

If the banjo notes sharp, move the bridge back toward the tail piece.

STRINGS

To get maximum volume and the best tone from your banjo, I suggest very light gauge strings. They are easier to note and seem to hold a good tone longer, for this style of playing.

The 1st, 2nd, 3rd and 5th strings should be plain steel (no wrapping). The 4th string should be wound or wrapped.

A good set of strings should last a month to six weeks without losing too much tone. A lot of people change and replace strings before they are actually worn out.

To preserve strings, wipe them clean after playing.

THE CAPO

A capo is used to clamp the first four strings down in order to play in different keys. This saves retuning of the first four strings.

The fifth, or short, string must be tuned up the same number of frets as the placement of the capo. Example: Capo placed at 4th — tune the 5th string 4 frets higher.

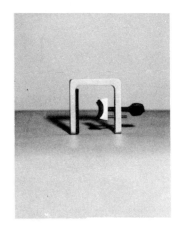

CHIMES

A banjo can be chimed in four places on the standard fingerboard. These are the 5th, 7th, 12th and 19th frets. The chimes on the 5th and 12th frets are in the key of G. The chimes on the 7th and 19th frets are in the key of D.

To chime — place the 3rd finger of the left hand, <u>lightly</u>, <u>across</u> <u>all</u> <u>five</u> strings at the desired fret. Barely touch the strings. When placed correctly, you can feel a string vibrate under your finger as it is picked with the right hand.

ROLLS

A <u>forward</u> roll is when the designated strings are played in a forward rotation. — thumb, index, middle, thumb, index, middle.

A <u>backward</u> roll would be the opposite. — thumb, middle, index, thumb, middle, index.

A <u>split</u> roll is a combination of parts or all or backward and forward rolls. — thumb, index, middle (forward) thumb, middle index (backward) put together.